26

HIMALAYAN ECO-SYSTEM DEVELOPMENT

Concept's Discovering Himalayas Series

No. 1. People's participation in Himalayan Eco-System Development **M.L. Dewan**

No. 2. Nut Fruits for the Himalayas **M.L. Dewan, M.C. Nautiyal** and **V.K. Sah**

No. 3. Vedic Philosophy for Himalayan Eco-system Development **M.L. Dewan** and **B.D. Joshi** (Eds.)

No. 4. Himalayan Eco-System Development : Impact of Fuelwood Plantation on Wastelands **R.D. Sharma**

ABOUT THE AUTHOR

DR. R.D. SHARMA holds M. Sc. (Ag.), Ph. D. degree in Agricultural Economics and specializes in farm economy research, rural development and project evaluation. He has long working experience under different capacities in India, Tanzania and Iraq. He is consultant to various organisations in Government of India and on the panel of experts with different international bodies. He has travelled widely in Africa, Middle East, South and East Asia under various assignments.

Dr. Sharma is the Founder-Director, Centre for Economic and Development Research, Ghaziabad and is associated with a number of academic institutions. He has to his credit over fifty publications.

By the same author

Economics of Fuelwood Production in Wastelands (Concept) 1992

Concept's Discovering Himalayas Series No. 4

HIMALAYAN ECO-SYSTEM DEVELOPMENT

Impact of Fuelwood Plantation on Wastelands

R.D. SHARMA

Director

Centre for Economic and Development Research,
Ghaziabad

CONCEPT PUBLISHING COMPANY, NEW DELHI 110059

ISBN 81-7022-520-5

First Published 1994

Ravindra D. Sharma (*b.* 1942)

Published and Printed by
Ashok Kumar Mittal
Concept Publishing Company
A/15-16, Commercial Block, Mohan Garden
NEW DELHI-110059

Lasertypeset by
Printing Express
H-13, Bali Nagar
NEW DELHI-110015

CONTENTS

LIST OF TABLES

LIST OF FIGURES

PREFACE

More than half of India's geographical area (329 million hectares) is estimated to be in various stages of degradation and 50 million hectares of this area have not been put to any productive use but these lands although wasted have the potential for development. Various organisations, in and outside the government have collected information on the Indian wastelands and some of the data thus collected are extremely useful for action plan at district level for the reclamation of wastelands through afforestation, socio and farm forestry, soil conservation and land management practices. It is being felt that an integrated approach for coordinated and realistic programme is needed for the development of eco-systems on these wastelands.

The various studies conducted in India have emphasised on different aspects of rural energy situation ranging from fuelwood supply and demand to the hard core problems being faced by the rural masses to get fuel within the reasonable distance of approach. The situation has become so alarming that the Planning Commission has estimated that the fuelwood availability would be one-third of its requirement by the turn of the century. The heavy burden on the drudgery rural people for fuelwood collection could not be removed unless fuelwood is not made available locally and comparatively cheap. Since land is a limited factor and agricultural lands are not available for fuelwood plantations, there has emerged the thinking to develop the country's wastelands into fuelwood and fodder plantations. This would, thus solve the two problems simultaneously, availability of fuelwood to the needy rural population and improving the eco-systems on these degraded lands.

The present study is aimed at developing fuelwood plantations on the wastelands so that the local eco-systems are improved through afforestation programme. The objectives of the study have been:

1. To collect information on the major eco-systems of the study area;
2. To examine the impact of plantations programme on the local rural population; and
3. To suggest propositions that benefit the local people and improve the eco-systems in the area.

To fulfil the above objectives, field investigations for the present study were conducted during 1991-92 in the State of Uttar Pradesh. District Pauri Garhwal–representing the Hill areas, and district Lakhimpur Khiri–representing the Plains, were selected on the basis of having maximum area under degraded lands besides the highest plantable area in the State. Three villages from the two districts were selected for field investigations. The data were collected from 260 households – 90 households from Hills and 170 households from Tarai plains.

The selected districts form a part of the Himalayan eco-system representing the foot-hills and Tarai zone of the region. Although geographically the two selected districts are located distant apart similarity in many characters of the system exists. Fauna, flora, land and water resources, cultural practices of the local people, etc, differ a lot in the studied area.

Emphasis was laid during the entire field investigations on the need to record the details of overall supply of resources from wastelands in the area. It was observed that fuelwoods are the major output from these degraded wastelands followed by fodder, small timber, etc. An assessment is made about the requirement and availability of fuelwoods to the local rural population. The other factors associated with this fuel supply resource were also studied in detail.

Fuelwood in the area under investigations contribute to about 70 per cent of the total energy needs of the households. Fuelwood utilization in the studied villages is recorded at about kgs 218,097 in the Hills and kgs 365,235 in the Tarai every year for domestic purposes. Almost all of this quantity is being used in kitchen for cooking purposes.

The Central as well as State governments have been participating in the programmes to popularize the smoke-less *chulhas* in the rural areas. Unfortunately, a very neg-ligible rural population have been adopting these fuelwood saving devices and their percentage is not even two per cent in the total households. As the primary motive in their design has been a desire to reduce the quantity of fuelwood used for cooking, i.e. to reduce the high level demand but their poor acceptability indicates that in the near future the fuelwood demand is not going to come down and hence it is expected that available fuelwood resources will further have the burden for overcutting.

Fuelwoods are being extensively used for all the cook-ing in the kitchen and rarely people depend on other fuels for their utilization. In the majority of households, twigs and dead trees are in use and are the common source of domestic energy supply. In Hill areas, only 11 per cent people have reported the use of logs. According to the data furnished, species such as *Pinus longifolic, Cedrela toona, Quercus incana* and *Grewia oppositifolia* in the Hill areas; and *eucalyptus, Dalbergia sissoo* and *Acacia spps.* in the Tarai plains suffer highest fuelwood load pressure.

About 16 per cent of the total fuelwood needs in the household sector come from own farm resources, i.e. through the plantations raised on farmer's lands. The forests contribute to about 21 per cent in the Hills and 7 per cent in the Tarai area of the total fuelwood supply. Community lands provide fuelwood supply to the tune of 63 per cent in the Hills, 29 per cent in the Tarai belt. Fuel-wood purchases are not common in the Hills but about one-fourth of the total requirement in the Tarai are being purchased either directly from markets or fellow villagers. Thus free collection in the Tarai belt has become scarce due to non-availability of fuelwoods in the surrounding areas.

Farmers of the Hill areas have not initiated any step towards the development of their degraded lands. In the Tarai area, 22 out of total 155 farmers have reported their participation in the process. During the first three years of land development activities in the Tarai, farmers have spent between Rs. 800 and Rs. 1,050 per household. The cost of this land development has paid the dividend. For the first three years, the rate of return from the lands so developed have been between Rs. 1,060 and Rs. 1,783 per household. The land improvement also has substantially provided employment to the participating farmers. The employment thus generated comes to about 45 days for males and 33 days for females per household.

The fuelwood shortages under this energy crises has generated the awareness about their cultivation by the farming community in the Tarai area. This has started resulting on the positive gains. Fuelwood trees have been planted on owned waste and farming lands. The farmers reported that a total of 2,120 trees on wastelands and 7,980 trees on agricultural lands (both under the block plantations and strip plantations) have been grown. Tree cultivation has not been an expensive job to the farmers. The raising cost per plant comes to Rs. 3.70 in both the cases of development.

Social forestry programme in the area has got momentum and local population have benefited through its employment oriented concept. The village people have substantially gained job opportunities in the plantation/afforestation programmes. In Hill areas, 635 days for males and 360 days for females were additionally provided by these projects. For the Tarai areas, the employment generated comes to 1,246 days for males and 107 days for females. Accordingly, the rural people have also benefited with the additional incomes to the family.

The utilization of domestic energy supplied with the fuelwoods in the households of the study area is being regulated by a number of socio-economic factors. A multiple linear regression relationship exists in between the total energy use and various countable and non-countable factors in the household. In the Hill areas, size of the household, non-agricultural incomes (especially the remittances) and rate of illiteracy have been found in positive correlation with the total domestic energy use. In the case of Tarai area, size of the household, agricultural incomes, and family maintenance expenditure have significant positive correlation with the energy use. It is interesting to note that the caste culture has no significant impact on the domestic use of fuelwood energy in both the areas.

Considering the demand and utilization of fuelwoods in the area, programme has been developed to improve the eco-system of the wasted lands by growing the energy plantations so that the fuelwood needs of the projected populations in 2001 is met. The programme is based on two criteria–separately for the landed households where farm forestry has to be taken up as part of crop/tree combination farming system and on the LMC wastelands for those households who do not have the land resources and hence have to depend for their fuelwood supplies on the government/village lands. According to the calculations provided in Section 6 of the book, while growing the most promising fuelwood species, there will be a short-fall of fuelwood on the landed class even in 2001. The village common lands, it is expected by that time will have the surplus produce. The majority of the households, thus who will be under the deficit stage by the beginning of the century, will be provided fuelwoods from the extra produce on the village wastelands. The production of fuelwoods on the village wastelands will not only suffice the need of the respective districts but will have sufficient marketable quantity of about 511,300 tonnes in Pauri district and 37,624 tonnes in Khiri district by the year 2001.

R.D. SHARMA

ACKNOWLEDGEMENTS

The author is thankful to Dr. B.S. Nagi, Council for Social Development, New Delhi, Dr. A.R. Nautiyal, High Altitude Plant Physiology Research Centre, H.N.B. University Garhwal, Srinagar, and Dr. Iqbal Singh, Indian Agriculture Research Institute, New Delhi, for their help and assistance provided for the completion of the study.

The author is also thankful to Indian Council of Social Science Research, New Delhi, for providing research grant to the study.

ENERGY CALCULATIONS

The Domestic Fuelwood Energy Consumption include:

- For family cooking
- Annual feasts including religious functions
- Ceremonial purposes, like marriage celebration feasts, death feasts, etc.; and
- Post-harvest agricultural technologies like boiling of rice before pounding etc.

Conversion Ratios used
(Energy in terms of Mega Joule)

1. Dung cakes : kgs x 8.75368
2. Agricultural Waste : kgs x 11.25575
3. Fuelwood : kgs x 12.36895
4. Soft Coke : kgs x 22.97016
5. Kerosene oil : lts x 45.93474

GLOSSARY

Afforestation	:	Forest established artificially on the land which previously did not carry forests.
Agro-forestry	:	A sustainable land management system which increases the yield of the land, combines the production of crops (including tree crops) and forest plants and/or animals simultaneously or sequentially on the same unit of land and applied management practices that are compatible with the cultural practices of the local population.
Angithi/sigri	:	Portable *chulha* generally made of used iron packing materials e.g., buckets, tin, etc.
Biomass	:	Comprises all forms of matter derived from the biological activities taking place either on the surface of the soil or at different depths of the vast body of water lakes, streams, rivers, seas and oceans.
Block Plantations	:	Planting of forestry trees in fields–both as pure cultivation or inter-cropped with the field crops.
Border Plantations		Planting of forestry trees on the boundaries of farm fields.

Community Forestry : Any situation which ultimately involves local people in a forestry activity.

Conventional Fuel or Commercial Energy : Sources of energy which are available after paying against money. These sources are channelled through proper marketing system e.g. coal, petroleum, etc,

Coppicing : The ability to regenerate by shoots or root suckers of trees coming out after cutting of the stem of the trees above the ground level or a forest so established.

Dry wood : Fuelwood used for energy purposes in the form of air-dry stage.

Dung cake : Sun dried cakes made of cow/buffalo dung used extensively all over India as a major source of energy in the villages.

Eco-systems : All the communities in a given area, considered together with their non-living environment. In general, an eco-system is a reasonably recognizable area, although adjacent eco-system can overlap.

Energy Consumption : Fuelwood consumption by multiplying by the calorific value of the fuel (MJ/kg) is converted into the units of energy consumption.

Energy Forestry : Afforestation with the objective to maximise the woody biomass.

Environment	: The surrounding condition and/or forces that influence or modify (i) the whole complex of climate edaphic and biotic factors that act upon an organism or an ecological community and ultimately determine its form and survival, and (ii) the aggregate of social and cultural conditions that influence the life of an individual and community.
Fuelwood	: The terms 'fire wood' and 'fuelwood' are generally used interchangeably, 'fire wood' cannotes small-scale use such as for home cooking whereas 'fuelwood' implies large scale industrial use.
Fuel Consumption	: The amount of fuel consumed during the cooking. For this measurement, fuel available to the cook is pre-weighted and fuel remaining upon the completion of the meal is weighted in order to obtain the consumption during cooking.
Joule(J)	: The smallest unit of energy adopted internationally in place of calorie as a unit of measurement for heat energy. One calorie equals to 4.184 Joule.
LMC or Village Commonlands	: Gram Panchayat lands under panchayat ownership but panchayats have limited rights to transfer these lands.

Non-commercial Energy/ non-Conventional Fuels	:	Sources of energy available for its supply without paying cash, e.g. dung cakes, firewood, agricultural wastes, etc.
Improved *Chulha*	:	Synonymously used for smokeless *chulha*.
Open *Chulha*	:	Hearth generally made of mud, stones or bricks used for cooking the meals.
Plantable area	:	The area of the wastelands that could be brought under tree plantation programme.
Social Forestry	:	The practice of forestry in all its aspects on farms and village common lands (LMC) generally integrated with other farm operations.
Strip Plantations	:	Tree cultivation programme taken up on the side of railways, roads, canals, rivers, etc. Strip plantation is some times called as linear plantations.
Vegetable/agricultural waste and crop residues	:	Residues of field crops (tops, roots, shoots, bark, etc,) generally used as a source of non-conventional energy.
Wastelands	:	The term is being used as synonym of degraded lands. It is a general term which includes any type of land, irrespective of its ownership, which is producing less then 20 per cent of its optimum biological productivity.

1

INTRODUCTION

The total geographical area of India is 329 million hectares. Of this total area, 143 million hectares constitute agricultural lands and 67 million hectares forest lands. A large part of these lands are suffering from varying degrees of soil degradation. This degradation has been due to ceaseless onslaughts of lands in the last few decades. The relentless pressure of an increasing human and cattle population, the diversion of lands in fragile eco-systems for dams and roads, urbanisation, the destruction of forest wealth through reckless exploitation by contractors, faulty expansion of irrigation systems, improper agricultural practices on marginal lands etc, have all caused a level of degradation. The main causes of this degradation have been through the sheet erosion, stream erosion, shifting cultivation, sand dune movements, etc. Estimates are that approximately, 175 million hectares, more than half of India is degraded, whose productivity is far below its potential.[1] The significance of these degraded wastelands are thus largely man made and cause misery to millions of rural poor.

Fuelwood shortages have been acute with increase in population on the one hand and decreasing forests on the other hand. Increased intensity of floods and droughts have added to the shortages. The famine and misery drought, force the poor to cut the remaining surviving trees to earn a quick gain in the market. According to the existing forest policy, 33 per cent of the country should be the forest. Today, on paper about 23 per cent is forest but in reality good forest cover is perhaps only 11 per cent.[2] This 11 per cent is under continuous pressure to supply a population with forest produce way in excess of its capacity. According to the Planning Commission estimates, by the turn of the century the demand for fuelwood would be about three times of the expected supply.[3] Thus there is growing gap between demand and availability of fuelwoods. These shortages lead to very severe overexploitation of the forests leading to further degradation and destruction. The first study utilising satellite imagery data shows that about 1.5 million hectares of forests are being lost every year.[4] On these grounds it is easy to see that at this rate, our remaining 30 odd million hectares of natural forests are likely to be completely depleted within another decade or two. If this is allowed to happen, we shall be facing an ecological and economic disaster from which it will be impossible to recover.

Crop production on wastelands is not economic at all. Considering the poor productivity of these lands, nature of risk involved, employment potential, demand for the output, and overall economic gains, introduction of fuel/commercial wood plantations seems to be the most appropriate technology for wasteland development and utilisation. Realising this, the emphasis was given that the tree plantation having specific characteristics be urgently taken up on these degraded wasteland. These included nitrogen fixing ability, rapid growth, ability to coppice, ability to produce wood of high calorific value that burns without spark to toxic smoke and ability to grow in a wide range of environments including different altitudes, soil types, rainfall regimes, amount of sunlight and terrain.[5]

The Government of India and different State Governments have taken up a number of projects in collaboration with the international donor agencies like CIDA, USAID, World Bank, SIDA, etc, for a massive national afforestation programme.[6] The main objectives of these projects are that the afforestation of wastelands will bring immediate benefit in terms of rural employment and the plantation will make the basic needs of the rural population available and will also encourage wood based cottage industries. The afforestation will also help in conserving the existing forests on which human and cattle pressure will reduce to a considerable extent. Pasture development will provide for grazing needs of local livestock and productivity will increase as a result of introduction of management systems leading to land improvement.

Energy has also become a critical input, and a major constraint is sustainable agriculture and rural development, since the first oil price adjustment in the early 1970's, which brought in its wake shortages of all forms of commercial energy. The commercial energy shortages, combined with the "other energy crises" caused by the continued dependence of the rural people, on the rapidly dwindling non-commercial biomass resources of fuelwood, crop residues and dung cakes have hit the rural areas in the country hardest. The rural energy crisis, has been getting increasing attention from the policy and in the Seventh Five-Year Plan (1985-1990) an attempt was made to tackle this problem in a planned and integrated manner. This was because it affects the very survival of the vast majority of the country's population, who live in the rural areas, and is also deeply inter-linked with the whole concept of sustainable development.

In India, agriculture, for example, contributes to the major proportion of national income (35%) and provides employment for more than two-thirds the work force (70%), gets 12 per cent[7] of total commercial energy. The growth of other non-agricultural income-generating activities which have the potential for providing employment to the growing labour force and stem large scale rural/urban migration, is often seriously constrained due to the scarcity of commercial energy for rural development. Also, the energy in rural areas is used mainly for household consumption. These household energy needs are met by 'non-commercial' energy sources which are secured by private efforts at almost zero cost. For their survival, the rural people have to get these since there are no other alternatives in the rural areas. Thus, economic and fiscal sanctions, and legal and administrative measures make little impact in controlling the damage that is being caused to the environment by the continuing, widespread and often unsustainable use of these resources.

Methodology

The field investigations for the present study were conducted in the State of Uttar Pradesh. Social forestry programme in the State has been initiated with the assistance of World Bank. The programme on wasteland reclamation in the State of Uttar Pradesh was started in 1950-51. This included reclamation of fallow as well as alkalic soils and the programme was directed mainly to agricultural areas. During the period 1974-75 and 1981-82, 65,900 hectares of sodic soils especially for the purpose of tree plantations were reclaimed in the State. The latest data upto 1989-90 show that about 40,000 hectares of tree plantations under the social forestry are raised in the State every year. Besides, about 2,550 lakh seedlings per year are distributed through the farm forestry programme. Uttar Pradesh stands next only to Madhya Pradesh and Maharashtra in social forestry plantations and tops the rank for the farm forestry programme in India.[8]

For the purpose of micro level investigations, two districts – one from hills and another from plains, were selected. The criterion of selection for the districts has been the maximum area under the wastelands that can be available for development and the largest area covered under tree plantations during the last five-year period.

The 1985-86 has been considered the base year for the use of secondary data. Uttar Pradesh has 56 districts in the base year while their number increased to 62 by 1989-90. Of the total districts in the State only 58 have got vacant lands (used synonymously for wastelands) ranging between 115 hectares in district Basti and 121,433 hectares in Pauri Garhwal. The total area of these wastelands in the State accounts for 8,72,127.87 hectares. Due to certain constraints, all these vacant lands could not be available for development; hence for plantations 24 districts of the State fall under the category where no lands are available for plantations. According to the State Government estimates, the total plantable area comes to about 3,55,477 hectares, divided as 2,96,165 hectares under the plains and 5,9312 hectares in the hills.[9]

The districtwise break-up of total plantable area in the State shows that in plains Unnao has got the maximum, 33,148 hectares and Bijnore lowest acreage only 108 hectares. Under the hill districts, Chamoli ranks first having 30,912 hectares of plantable area while Almora and Tehri Garhwal have no such area. Considering all the countable and non-countable factors, districts of Pauri Garhwal from hills and Lakhim Pur Khiri from plains are selected for field investigations. The respective areas of the above described lands in the two districts are shown in Table 1.1:

TABLE 1.1: Wastelands and Plantable Area in the Selected Districts

District	Wastelands (ha)	Plantable (ha)	Percentage of Plantable area to Wastelands
Pauri Garhwal	121,433.41	18,245.38	15.03
Lakhimpur Khiri	11,686.60	9,261.60	79.25
Uttar Pradesh	8,72,127.87	3,55,477.37	40.76

Source : Department of Forests, Uttar Pradesh, Lucknow.

Plantations of various species under different programmes and schemes are raised in all the districts of Uttar Pradesh. During the five-year period (1985-86 to 1989-90) 4,05,669 hectares of land was covered under these plantations. The yearwise break-up is given in Table 1.2.

There have been variations in the planted area for different districts and years. The hill districts of the State have extensively been planted from the viewpoint of acreage. District of Pauri Garhwal with 46,424 hectares planted area tops the list. In the plains, wide variations in planted area are reported. Lakhim Pur Khiri, Mirza Pur and Behraich districts have the largest area planted during this period. The area planted in each of these districts fall a little over 9,000 hectares. The annual area planted in the two selected districts is given in Table 1.3.

TABLE 1.2: Annual Plantations Raised in Uttar Pradesh

Year	Area Planted (ha)
1985-86	64,244
1986-87	77,477
1987-88	87,985
1988-89	92,693
1989-90	83,270
Total	405,669

Source: Department of Forests, Uttar Pradesh, Lucknow.

TABLE 1.3: Planted Area Under Various Species in the Selected Districts

Year	Area Planted (ha)	
	Pauri Garhwal	Lakhim Pur Khiri
1985-86	7,110.00	1,619.00
1986-87	8,826.44	1,303.00
1987-88	10,666.61	1,872.00
1988-89	11,784.00	2,002.00
1989-90	8,037.00	2,380.50
Total	46,424.06	9,176.50

Source: Department of Forests, Uttar Pradesh, Lucknow.

On the basis of the criterion laid down for selecting the districts, two villages–one each from the two districts was selected for detailed field enquiry. Considering the small size of village Dang, selected in district Pauri Garhwal, an adjoining village Agrora was also investigated to broaden the coverage of the households. Although the two villages have their own identity and settlements but for the purpose of the present study the two have been considered as a single village unit. The villages have a common land boundary and fall in the same eco-system. These two villages come under the Kalji Khal Development Block. Village Rukandipur of block and district Lakhim Pur Khiri was selected to represent the field enquiry from the plain areas.[10]

The Study Area

The two selected districts are located in the north-central parts of Uttar Pradesh. Pauri Garhwal forms a part of Garhwal Division while Lakhim Pur Khiri comes under the Lucknow division. These two districts vary from physical features to socio-economic culture and are distinctly identified in nature.

District Pauri Garhwal as a part of hilly tract of Himalayas, is also the headquarters district of Garhwal Division. It lies between 29.20° and 30.15° north of equator and 78.10° and 79.20° to the east. The northern boundary is with district Chamoli, in east districts of Almora and Nainital, Bijnore in the south and districts of Dehradun and Tehri in the west.

The total geographical area of the district is 5,440 sq. kms and except part of southern Bhabar belt, river banks and Sri Nagar area, whole of the district comes under the mountainous terrain with valleys and altitude ranging between 900 to 2,250 metres.

The annual rainfall is about 1,545 m.m. with maximum temperature 31.7°C in May and minimum below zero degree in January. Alaknanda, Nayar's, Nalini, Khoh are the main and perennial rivers while other smaller and seasonal rivers of the district are Ram Ganga, Rewasan etc. The whole of the district is rich in fauna and flora, having various species of commercial importance.

District Pauri is divided into five tehsils, namely, Pauri, Kotdwar, Lansdown, Thalisen and Dhuna Kot. The tehsils are further divided into 15 development blocks. There are 3,237 inhabited villages in the district. According to 1981 census, district Pauri has got 6,37,877 persons. Females outnumber the males and there are 1,091 females after every 1,000 male population. The entire district has rural character making over 90 per cent of the population living in the villages. The rate of population growth during the last decade (1971-80) has been 11.7 per cent. Average household size in the district is of 5 persons.

District Lakhim Pur Khiri falls partly under the Tarai belt of north–central Uttar Pradesh. It lies between 27.6° and 28.6° north of equator and 80.34° and 81.3° to the east. The northern boundary of the district is with Nepal, in the east district Behraich, in south districts of Hardoi and Sitapur and in the west with districts Shajahan Pur and Pilibhit.

The total geographical area of the district is 7,680 sq kms. The major part of the district falls under the grasses of Tarai belt and forests towards the northern side while south wards intensive agriculture is practised on irrigation pattern. The terrain of the district is almost flat with slope towards the east.

The major rivers that flow in the district are Ghagra, Kodiyala, Saryu, Sharda, Gomti etc. Northern parts of the district due to massive river system and poor drainage are waterlogged for most of the rainy season and partially cut off from rest of the district. Average annual rainfall is about 1,445.6 m.m. Maximum temperature touches upto 44°C in summer (May and June) while fog is very common during the winter season.

District Khiri from administrative point of view is divided into tehsils, namely, Lakhim Pur, Mohammadi, Gola Gokarn nath, Nidhasan and Dhorhara. There are 15 development blocks and 1,699 inhabited villages in the district. According to 1981 census, the district Khiri has got 19,52,700 persons with 846 females after every 1,000 males. About 90.4 per cent of the district's population live in the villages. The rate of population growth in the district during the 1971-81 decade has been 31.34 per cent. Average household size comes to 5.52 persons.

Table 1.4 gives a comparative information about the two districts.

The Selected Villages

1. *Dang and Agrora*

Villages Dang and Agrora are situated about 16 kms, from

district headquarters Pauri towards south in the Kalzikhal block. According to 1981 census, the two villages together have 563 persons living in 82 households (Dang 39 households with 271 persons and Agrora 43 households with 292 persons). Contrary to the district figures, the ratio of males to total population is higher in the village. They account about 1,014 for every 1,000 females. About 47 per cent males and 23 per cent females of the villages are literates. The villages do not have population either of scheduled caste or scheduled tribe people.

TABLE 1.4: Basic Data for the Two Selected Districts

Items/Categories	District Khiri	District Pauri
Population density/sq. kilometer (1981)	276.0	105.0
Percentage of SC/ST to total population (1981)	28.9	12.0
Percentage of workers to total population (1981)	31.7	36.4
Percentage of workers in agriculture to total workers (1981)	94.7	80.5
Literacy (%) (1981)	15.1	38.5
Area under cereals to total cropped area (%) (1987-88)	65.1	95.9
Cropping intensity (%) (1987-88)	134.4	152.4
Use of fertilizers per cropped ha (kg.) (1987-88)	54.5	3.3
Foodgrains Production/Capita in kg. (1987-88)	340.0	321.0
Per cropped hectare value of products on current prices (Rs.) (1987-88)	6358.0	1720.0
Net irrigated area to total irrigated area (%) (1987-88)	129.9	124.1
Net irrigated area to net cropped area (%) (1987-88)	45.5	6.4
Canal irrigated area to total irrigated area (%) (1987-88)	14.6	33.1
Tubewell irrigated to total irrigated area (%) (1987-88)	85.0	3.1
Gobar gas plants per 100 villages (1988-89)	156.0	12.5
Electrified villages to total villages (%) (1988-89)	70.2	50.3
Wastelands per person (ha)	0.04	0.13
Forest area per person (ha)	0.08	0.71

Source: District Statistical Bulletins, Pauri and Khiri, 1989.

Dang according to the village records has 92 hectares of land area while Agrora has got 65 hectares. The forest area accounts for 7 hectares and 4 hectares in the two villages respectively. Each village has got half hectare of irrigated land. Of the total cropped area in the two villages, unirrigated area accounts for 45 hectares in Dang and 40 hectares in Agrora. Quite a large area of the villages are lying under the culturable waste: 25 hectares in Dang and 8 hectares in Agrora. Rice and wheat are the staple food of the local people in the villages.

2. *Rukundipur*

Village Rukundipur is situated on Khiri-Gola road and about 13 kms towards west from Khiri. According to 1981 census, the total population of the village was 1,129 persons inhabited in 147 households. Of the total population, 691 are males and 438 females. About 39.65 per cent males and 5.02 per cent females are literate in the village. Forty per cent of the population belong to scheduled caste. Of the 452 total male workers, cultivators account for over 65 per cent in the village and form the bulk of the working class people engaged in agriculture and allied works – the main profession in the village.

Rukundipur, according to the village records has 370.30 hectares of land area. Of the total cultivated area of 278.3 hectares, 174.7 hectares are irrigated (141.11 hectares by government canals, 32.78 hectares by tube wells and 0.81 hectare by tanks) and rest 103.60 hectares are unirrigated. The cultivable wastelands account for 39.36 hectares (10.63 per cent) and area not available for agricultural purposes is 52.61 hectares.

Wheat and rice are the staple food of the people and sugarcane is the major cash crop grown intensively in village. Wells and hand pumps are the sources of drinking water. The village has got a primary school while medical aid, post office, local market, railway station and veterinary hospital are located at a distance of about 5 kilometers.

Field Approach and the Studied Households

The two districts and the three villages surveyed therein were selected on a criterion mentioned in the earlier section of the book. Local enumerators were selected and hired to carry out the field investigations. The selection of the enumerators was from the High Altitude Plant Physiological Research Centre, HNB, Garhwal University, Sri Nagar, for investigations in the villages of Pauri district, i.e. for hill areas, and from a Lakhimpur Khiri based voluntary organisation for Khiri district, i.e. for Tarai area. This was mainly done to facilitate the local dialects of languages in use within households and especially among the females. Enumerators were given short training about the data collection including the usage of various fuels, fodder, etc. and in filling the questionnaires. The pre-testing of schedules was done locally. All the inhabited households of the three villages were covered in the survey. The field survey was applied at two points in time during 1991-92 and the major source of information have been the female folk of the households. In a few of the cases, to counter check the data collected, enumerators were asked to weigh the fuels, fodder which was actually used in the household.

At the CEDR's headquarters questionnaires were developed. After testing, the questionnaires were modified and the completed ones were further checked and arranged for computer processing of data. The computer processing of the data was done at the Council for Social Development, New Delhi.

TABLE 1.5: Details of the Households Covered in the Study

Description	Hills		Tarai	
	Unit	Percentage	Unit	Percentage
1	2	3	4	5
Total households	90	34.6	170	65.4
Caste composition of households				
(i) Upper Caste	90	100.0	21	12.4
(ii) Backwards	–	–	94	55.3
(iii) SC+ST	–	–	55	32.4

(Contd.)

TABLE 1.5 (*Contd.*)

1	2	3	4	5
Religion of the households				
(i) Hindu	90	100.0	143	84.1
(ii) Muslim	—	—	26	15.3
(iii) Sikh	—	—	1	0.6
Sex composition of the households				+
Males				
(i) Children below 12 years	1.25	—	1.43	—
(ii) All	3.31	—	4.76	—
Females				
(i) Children below 12 years	1.45	—	1.36	—
(ii) All	3.22	—	3.21	—
Household Size	6.53	—	7.93	
Literacy in the households				
(i) Illiterates	1.90	29.10	3.09	38.97
(ii) Literates	4.63	70.90	4.84	61.03
Total population of the household				+
(i) Males	298	50.68	810.0	60.00
(ii) Females	290	49.32	540.0	40.00
Total	588	100.00	1350.0	100.0
Level of the Head of the household				
(i) Under 30 years	13	14.44	18	10.59
(ii) 31-41 years	27	30.00	44	25.88
(iii) 41-50 years	20	22.22	54	31.76
(iv) 51-60 years	12	13.33	45	26.47
(v) 61-over	18	20.00	9	5.29
Total	90	100.00	170	100.00
Livestock raising in the households				
(i) With livestock	84	93.33	129	75.88
(ii) Without livestock	6	6.67	41	24.12
Total	90	100.00	170	100.00
Total Livestock population				
(i) Buffaloes	41	11.05	112	19.86
(ii) Cows	194	52.29	121	21.45
(iii) Bullocks	62	16.71	62	10.99
(iv) Goats & Sheep	17	4.58	203	35.99
(v) Others	57	15.36	66	11.70
Total	371	100.00	564	100.00

(*Contd.*)

TABLE 1.5 (*Contd.*)

1	2	3	4	5
Households with				
(i) Land	84	93.33	155	91.18
(ii) Without land	6	6.67	15	8.82
Average size of the holding (hectare)	0.7	–	2.40	–
Irrigated area per holding (hectare)	Neg.	–	1.40	–
Percentage of irrigated area to total holding area	16.28	–	58.42	–
Total cropped area (hectare)	58.00	–	377.00	–
Total land possessed by the studied households (hectares)				
(i) Wheat	27	–	66	–
(ii) Paddy	23	–	44	–
(iii) Sugarcane	–	–	241	–

NOTES

1. NWDB, First Meeting of the National Land Use and Wastelands Development Council, New Delhi, 1986.
2. NWDB, Wastelands Development Programmes, Guidelines for Action, New Delhi, 1985.
3. Planning Commission, Report of the Fuelwood Study Committee, New Delhi, 1982.
4. Kamla Chowdhry, *Wastelands and the Rural Poor*, New Delhi, 1987.
5. Vimal, O.P. and Tyagi, P.D., *Bio-Energy from Wastelands*, New Delhi, 1986.
6. Bentley, W., The Uncultivated Half, USAID Report, Ford Foundation, New Delhi, 1984.
7. S.K. Chopra, Survey of Indian Agriculture, *The Hindu*, Madras, 1988.
8. Indian Agriculture in Brief, 20th Edition, Ministry of Agriculture, New Delhi.
9. Districts of Nainital, Almora, Pithoragarh, Pauri Garhwal, Tehri Garhwal, Uttar Kashi, Chamoli and Dehra Dun form hill parts of the State.
10. Plains are a very broad and wide concept. Particularly as regards the State of Uttar Pradesh is concerned, they varied according to the nature and agro-climatical conditions from north to south and west to east. With the present context, the plains of the selected district Lakim Pur Khiri are climatically more close to the Tarai characteristics. And hence to differentiate them with the broad term word *Tarai* in this report has been adopted for explanations.

2

MAJOR ECO-SYSTEMS OF THE STUDY AREA

Estimates have shown that fuelwood accounts for nearly four-fifths of the energy needs of most of the rural families and about half of the urban families in India. The seriousness of the problem of fuelwood shortages has more emerged after the oil crises in 1973. Considering the situation to be faced in the beginning of the next century the Government of India have taken various steps for the afforestation programme. The social forestry concept has also taken the form of energy forestry and a lot of work as is reported has been made on the generation of fuelwood resources. The reasons for the failure of these programmes may be many, but one important reason is the fact that fuelwood is involved in a number of relationships and there is insufficient appreciation of either the nature of extent of these relationships.

Since the fuelwood cannot be cultivated in an isolated manner, there are a lot of factors involved in the process. The whole of the process comes under the development of eco-systems pattern. The environmental constraints, economic activities of the local people, their interaction, etc, play a major role in the development of wood energy programmes in a particular given agricultural/forest eco-systems.

Pauri Garhwal and Lakhim Pur Khiri, the two study districts, although geographically not very far away from each other, differ in a number of characteristics. As already has been disclosed in the earlier section, the observed differences are noticed in natural resources, fauna and flora besides the cultural practices of the local population. The major systems are discussed below.

District Pauri Garhwal

Land Resources

The district of Pauri comprises three distinct physical features; Tarai Bhabar, foot-hills (Siwalik zone or sub-Himalayas as occasionally they call) and lower Himalayas.

The Tarai Bhabar is the southernmost part of the district bordering with district of Bijnore. The Tarai, a broad belt of over 15 kilometers wide and 95 kilometers long, extends from Ganga in the west to Ramganga in the east. The elevation varies and between 300 and 600 meters at various places. The Khoh river divides the Tarai Bhabar into western (Kotdwara Bhabar) and eastern (Kalagarh Bhabar) parts. Tarai belt is extensively covered with grassy and swampy plains, marshes and fans, oozing streams and water choked morasses.

The foot-hills rising to about 1,000 meters in height and lying just north of the Tarai belt. The zone is divided into number of hills. The average width varies from a few kilometers to about 15 kilometers. The foot-hills are made up of fresh water deposits composed mostly of clay, sandstone, grits and consolidation and yield considerable sediment during heavy rains.

North of the foot-hills region lies the lower Himalayas. These vary in width upto 50 kilometers and are profusely dissected, forming a mass of peaks rising upto 3,000-4,000 meters. The Nayar basin, Alaknanda basin and Dudhatoli range are the main mountain ranges of the district. These basins consist of a chain of hill ranges and the valleys. The valleys are carved out by the small seasonal streams and comprises narrow flat lands, bordered by a series of terraces and are being used for agriculture both under irrigation and dry farming. Dudhatoli range with mean elevation of over 1,800 meters is a plateau possessing summit high flat land and relatively gentler slopes with rich cover of grass and grazing lands.

The soils of Pauri district are highly varied in keeping

with the topographic and climatic variations. They are shallow, coarse and stoney on the upper parts of the slopes gradually changing to moderately deep and finer textured down slope to deep fine loams or silt clays in the valley bottoms. The soil structure is generally weak especially on slopes. The organic content is also low and varies to a great extent. They have dark brown to red colour at different places. A large part of the district soils have no value or no agricultural value and offer scope for only grazing. Dry farming on the terraced slopes is a common feature of cultivation throughout the district. The river beds and valleys have a small area under irrigation farming.

Wastelands cover a large part of the district and they account for about 12 per cent of the total reporting area. The major wasteland groups are in the form of cultivable wastelands (36,207 hectares), fallow lands (15,103 hectares) and wastelands not good for agricultural purposes (291,911) hectares). The availability of these wastelands according to their ownership rights, etc., is far below than the area mentioned under the above three categories. It has been ascertained that only about 18,000 hectares of the above could be available for development either for afforestations or for the orchards etc. Unfortunately, no data are available on these wastelands, but with the opinion collected from the people who are familiar with the local situation, over half of these wastelands now stands without any cover and coverless land areas are increasing in a very rapid way. In the majority of cases, the slopes above villages, area of civil or '*soyam*' lands which were demarcated for wood and grazing requirements of the villages, are now totally vanished and hardly have any cover. Other areas near the roads, etc, are also fast becoming coverless and will be main alarming patches in the near future for degradation.

The land utilization pattern based on the land records shows that out of the total geographical area of 7.33 lakh hectares in the district, about 61.36 per cent is under forests, and the remaining area is divided as: area available for cultivation 33.45 per cent, orchards 18.04 per cent, barren lands 15.63 per cent, grazing lands 14.64 per cent, lands put on non-agricultural uses 5.82 per cent, cultivable waste 12.78 per cent and net area sown 50.97 per cent. Table 2.1 gives the details of the district area.

TABLE 2.1: District Pauri–Land Utilisation

Category	Hectares	Land area	
		Percentages to	
		Total	Exal. forest area
Forests	4,50,012	61.36	—
Cultivable waste-lands	36,207	4.94	12.78
Fallow lands	15,103	2.06	5.33
Wastelands not good for agriculture	29,191	3.98	10.30
Other non-agricultural lands	16,503	2.25	5.82
Grazing lands	41,487	5.66	14.64
Orchards	51,111	6.97	18.04
Net cultivated area	94,779	12.92	33.45
Double cropped area	49,667	6.77	17.53
Net cropped area	1,44,446	19.70	50.97
Irrigated area	11,896	1.62	4.20

Source-: Statistical Bulletin–District Pauri, 1989 (Hindi Edition)

Due to climatically extreme and adverse topographical situation, district Pauri produces very limited crops. The main crops are wheat, small millets, rice and pulses. Table 2.2 gives the cropping pattern for the year 1987-88.

Water Resources

Pauri district is endowed with vast water resources. The major river system originating from higher Himalayas and/or Dudhatoli range contributes a lot to the natural water system including the drainage pattern. The main rivers are Alaknanda, western and eastern Nayar, Ramganga, Khoh and Huinal and their tributaries. These rivers also drain most part of the district. Besides the sufficient number of rivers in the district the surface water has not been properly and tapped there is shortage of groundwater due to the hilly topography of the area. Whatever water is available through natural springs is being used for irrigation and drinking purposes. The groundwater depth is about 100 meters on an average in the Tarai Bhabar area and attempts are being made by the government sources to tap it in a planned way. So far seven tubewells have been bored and are being used for irrigation purposes. Of the total irrigated area of about 12,000 hectares in the district; 47 per cent is by canals, 5 per cent by government tubewells and 48 per cent by private minor irrigation system. The total length of canals in the district comes to about 786 kilometers and these lie mainly in the Tarai belt. Hill cultivation, mainly on terraces is either under dry farming or through watering by small streams. There are 37 pump sets being used on streams besides 4,425 ponds and 902 kilometer length of stream channels in the hilly terrain of the district.

TABLE 2.2: District Pauri—Cropping Pattern

Crops	Sown area	
	Hectare	Percentages
Wheat	41,336	28.62
Mandua	35,839	24.81
Paddy	25,143	17.41
Savan	21,753	15.06
Barley	8,616	5.96
Urad	2,307	1.60
Maize	2,148	1.49
Winter Pulses	1,464	1.01
Oil Seeds	749	0.52
Potatoes	258	0.18

Source : Statistical Bulletin—District Pauri, 1989 (Hindi Edition)

The drainage pattern, the run-off of the rivers, the rugged terrain and the sudden change in the levels as between the hills and plains are the basis for the potential use of surface water. But unfortunately, after the stoppage of the construction of Nayar dam at Marora near Satpuli in 1948, no sincere efforts are made to harness the potential of the major rivers in the district. Kalagarh dam is the only major project under construction in the southern part of the district. This dam after completion will be of least use to the local irrigation system in the district.

Forest Resources

The district Pauri has 450,012 hectares of forests which come to about 61 per cent of the total reported area. Of these forests about 55 per cent comes under reserved forests and the remaining 6 per cent under community forests. Most of the reserved forests lie in broad belt of Tarai Bhabar and its uplands stretching from the west to the east and on Dudhatoli range covering the north-eastern part of the district. Considering the only total geographical area reported for land utilization, community forests comprise 14 per cent of the area and are distributed throughout the district. According to the latest available statistics, the district forest area can be divided into:

Forest Departments	3,66,212 ha
Reserve Forests	2,39,902 ha
Civil Forests	1,80,600 ha
Panchayati Forests	29,640 ha
Private and Municipality Forests	607 ha

Under the Forest Department administration till 1989-90, an area of 3,66,212 hectares has been brought under their control. Of the total, the area under reserved forests comes to 239,902 hectares while the remaining area has got small bushes/shrubs or shrubs of less importance on the wastelands.

The distribution of altitudinal forests can easily be identified in the district of Pauri. Accordingly, the sub-tropical forests (below 1,200 meters) consist of a broad belt of Tarai Bhabar extending from Ganga in the west to Ramganga in the east besides at places in the Himalayas. These comprise the reserved forest of Gohri, Lasdang,

Kohtri, Palain, Sonanadi, Adnola, Mandal and south Patli Dun ranges. Further north of sub-tropical forests range lies the zone of temporate forests (1,200-1,800 meters,) containing thickly populated and intensively cultivated areas along the Nayar valleys. The sub-alpine forests (1,800-3,000 meters) covers the vast forest of Dudhatoli range exceeding over hundreds of square kilometers.

The forests of Pauri district produce a large variety of both major and minor products. Timber, fuelwood and fodder constitute the major products while minor products are Katha, resin, lime, limestone, gypsum, bamboos, canes etc., The main species (local names in the brackets) found in the district forests are:

Sub-tropical forests :

Shorea robusta	(Sal)
Dalbergia sissoo	(Shisham)
Salmalia malabrica	(Simol)
Acacia catechu	(Khair)
Cedrela toona	(Tun)
Bamboos	(Bans)

Temporate Forests :

Pinus longifolia	(Chir)
Cedrela toona	(Tun)
Enginia dallierglodes	(Sandan)
Rhododen drenarborem	(Binao)
Quercus incana	(Oak, Bhanj)
Emblica officinalis	(Anwala)
Grewia oppositifolia	(Bhimal)
Cedrus deodara	(Deoder)
Adina cordifolia	(Haldu)
Rosa moschatta	(Kunja)
Rhus parviflora	(Tungla)
Boehmeria rugulosa	

Sub-alpine forests :

Querous incaus	(Bhanj)
Querous diatotes	(Tilong)
Querous semicaipifolia	(Kharsoo)

Berberies asiatica	(Kilnora)
Rosa moschatta	(Kunja)
Bamboos	(Bans)

The present state of degradation in some of the areas of forests is a serious one in the district. There have been a number of factors behind these but the introduction of *zamindari* system in the long past by British has been the most important. According to this system, the ancient tenure pattern was changed which destroyed the community organisation. The village forests under the community control has been maintained on a sustainable basis. The *zamindars* were only too anxious to make money as fast as possible out of their new acquisitions. In pursuance of this policy, the *zamindars* prohibited the tenants from grazing and cutting wood in village forests and sold the latter to charcoal burners who completely denuded the hillsides. In fact the whole of the hill region was devastated of timber. The Indian Forests Act was brought into effect to generate timber for future uses. This laid the basis for present situation, for it restricted the area of forest and grazing land for the local people and left it under the district administration. These so called 'Civil' or 'Soyam' forests are now the most degraded areas of the district.

This is on these lands that under forestry programme, afforestation is taking place. Under various schemes in this head, afforestation on 10,406 hectares on degraded lands have been done during the year 1989-90.

In the whole of Pauri district, the domestic consumption of fuelwood is preponderant. In the long winter season, the need to keep warm increases energy requirement which is greater than that during the summer season. The fuelwood for this requirement represents almost all the energy resources. The major sources of fuelwood in the district include government forests 'Soyam' or 'Civil' forests, fuelwood plantations and natural wood such as raw plantations, hedges, village wood lots, orchards and trees scattered over the arable land. Due to population pressure and other countable factors, the fuelwood consumption in the district in recent years has increased than the level of supply compatible with sustained production. Hence, there is almost overcutting of wooded lots resulting in serious erosion.

Livestock and Grazing Resources

According to the 1982 livestock census, the Pauri district has about 682,000 heads of livestock. The major livestock categories are cows (381,185), buffaloes (71,218), sheep (48,828) and goats (179,080). The land utilization district data show that 41,487 hectares of land fall under the categories of grazing lands. This area is about 8 per cent of the total reporting area. According to these statistics, the cattle population on 100 hectares of the reporting area comes to 93 and for 1,000 persons it is only 1.59. The milch cattle per 100 persons comes to 30 in the district. On an average about 16 heads of livestock come per hectare of grazing land. Since the practice of tying up the cattle and providing chaffed fodder is not followed in the district, almost all the livestock go for grazing. Herding is not common in the district. Cattle owners generally leave their livestock for free grazing in the morning and by evening without any follow up they return to their homes. A very common practice observed in the district is to store fodder on the top of trees (fodder may be grasses or straw). This is generally done to save the fodder from moisture and untimely eating by the cattle. The stored fodder is used as buffer stock for dry season and generally served without chaffing.

The increased pressure of population, limited cultivated area and demand for milk and milk products in the district, have forced the cultivators to convert the limited grazing lands into farming patches. This trend has recently been observed in almost all geographical locations of the Pauri district. This has not only converted erstwhile grass patches (destroying grazing areas) into farm land on the higher Himalayas but has also caused reduction of the vegetation cover protecting steep slopes from the risk of excessive soil erosion.

The grazing land eco-system of the Pauri district are mostly formations which have been substituted for forest climax. A common feature is the predominance of various species of grasses leading to re-establishment of natural vegetation in abandoned farmed areas. The main species of fodder plants and grasses found in the district are:

Grewia oppositifolia
Chrysopogon aciculatus
Dialazium polypodiodies
Geranium wallichiana
Arundinella nepalensis
Poa alpina
Polypogon fugax
Potentilla sps.

Many of the above forest trees and particularly *Grewia oppositifolia* are heavily lopped for fodder in all seasons and throughout the district.

The encouragement of local people to establish their own forests for meeting their requirement through social forestry systems have helped a lot. Under the programme, trees are planted which produce fuel, fodder, fruits and other minor forest produce with grass and legumes in the interspace, which can be cut or when plantations are established, used for controlled grazing. Throughout the district many farmers practice a combined system of animal husbandry and agriculture and introduction of social forestry, i.e., integrated use of forests, grazing lands and crops is important for environmentally sound management, especially to protect water sheds and increase productivity of the fragile lands to meet the needs of the local population.

District Lakhim Pur Khiri

Land Resources

According to physical and geographical features, the district Khiri can be divided into two parts, Tarai or Ganjarand Uparhar.

The area bordering Sharda river in the north and Ghaghra river in the south is called Tarai. The total geographical area of this region is 2,709 square kilometers. The Tarai, forming rectangular in shape, is extensively covered with grasses and swampy plains. The northern part of Tarai has intensive forests which account for about 21 per cent of the total forest area of Khiri district. This forest area becomes, sparsely populated as one moves southwards. The area being close to Himalayas has maximum precipitation as compared to rest of the district and causing dense forests. In rainy season, most part of the Tarai area becomes huge water reservoir and looks like lakes and ponds. During the rainy and most part of the winter seasons, the Tarai region, containing mainly Tehsils of Nidhasan and Dhorhara are completely cut off from rest of the district. Means of communications are not well developed and absence of all weather roads including road bridges are the main cause of underdevelopment. The north-western part of Tarai, houses world famous Dudhawa National Park. The average altitude of Tarai area ranges between 150 and 180 meters.

The rest of the area of the district that falls south of river Sharda, is called Uparhar. It covers 4,982 sq. kilometers of the total geographical area of the district. The southern part of the Uparhar falls along the river Gomti. Uparhar is a flat area of plain lands with number of minor rivers and developed canal system of the Sharda tributaries. Most of the agricultural lands are irrigated either through canals or tubewells both government as well as private owned. Cropping intensity is high with wheat, sugarcane, paddy and oilseeds as the main crops.

Due to massive system of natural water courses, the soils of district Khiri, ranges between sandy and sandy loams. Most of the soils alongwith the river sides are sandy with less organic matter while major part of the district has fertile brown colour high with organic matter. Being a heavy flooded area, the texture of soils of the district used to change from time to time. Tarai area has silt and silty loam soils with dark brown colour and most suitable for growing sugarcane and paddy crops. *Toper* as is known, forms the major part of the soils of the district. These have light colour and sandy texture. Southern part of the district has loam soils with high fertility.

The district Khiri has about 9 per cent of its area under wastelands. The major groups of wastelands are found in the form of cultivable waste (6,618 hectares) fallow lands (54,920 hectares) and usar including other wastes (9,816 hectares). These categories account for 69.354 hectares of total wastelands in the district. The district has reported illegal possession on wastelands and quite a large part of these lands after reclamation is being used for cultivation, especially sugarcane farming. According to the data available, only 9,262 hectares of the wastelands in the district could be available for development under afforestation programme.

Unfortunately, details are not available but major part of these lands is under the waterlogging situation for most part of the year. The Tarai belt has got the maximum share and both the Tehsils of Dhorhara and Nidhasan suffer a lot especially during the rainy and winter seasons. Outside this belt wasteland area is being distributed under the *patta* system. There are fair chances to reclaim these lands and since the pH value is not so adverse, small amount of money invested per acre could be sufficient to make them fertile. Wastelands falling under the forest areas are being replanted with specified species suitable for timber and fuelwood.

The land utilization data based on village records show that district Khiri has a total of 770,076 hectares of land area. Out of this total reporting area about 21 per cent is under forests and of the remaining area the distribution is as: fallow lands 8.73 per cent, land put to non-agricultural uses 12.30 per cent, Usar 1.62 per cent, cultivable waste one per cent, orchards 1.15 per cent and net cultivated area 74.91 per cent. Table 2.3 gives the details of land utilization.

TABLE 2.3: District Khiri – Land Utilization

Category		Total area	
		Percentage to	
	Hectares	Total	Exc. forest area
Forests	1,63,749	21.26	–
Cultivable waste	6,618	0.86	1.09
Fallow lands	52,920	6.87	8.73
Usar	9,816	1.27	1.62
Area under non-agricultural uses	74,571	9.68	12.30
Grazing lands	1,277	0.17	2.12
Orchards	6,954	0.90	1.15
Net cultivated area	4,54,171	58.98	74.91
Total cropped area	6,10,550	79.28	100.70
Double cropped area	1,56,379	20.31	25.79
Irrigated area	2,06,485	26.81	34.06
Net irrigated area	2,68,311	34.84	44.25

Source : Statistical Bulletin–District Khiri, 1989, (Hindi Edition)

District Khiri produces a variety of crops. Due to developed irrigation system and the large area available under Tarai region, the cropping intensity is also high although it differs greatly from block to block. The main crops are sugarcane, wheat, paddy, oilseeds and maize. Table 2.4 gives the details of cropping pattern for the year 1989-90.

Water Resources

Like district Pauri, Lakhim Pur Khiri is also endowed with vast water resources. The major river systems of the district originate from the Himalayas and passing through the area contribute a lot to the natural water systems including the drainage pattern. The natural slope of the district is towards east. The main rivers are Mohan, Ghagra, Kodiyala, Saryu, Sharda, Ull, Sarayan, Chhoka, Gomti and Kathina. River Mohan forms the northern boundary of the district and separates India with Nepal and towards the east it merges with Ghagra (Kodiyala). Mohan changes its flow sometimes in India and at others in Nepal. Due to its changing flow a large part of the Dhorhara and Nidhasan tehsils has become lakes and ponds. Waterlogging has been a perennial problem of these Tehsils. River Sharda divides the district into two parts–the northern and southern. These two parts differ greatly in climate and also in the livings of the local people. Ghaghra, Sharda and Gomti, the three major rivers of the district, spread into vast areas in the rainy season, create floods and are the main causes of yearly damages of property, crops and human life. In the absence of proper drainage system in the northern part of the district, the area for most months of the year remain isolated with the rest of the district. The total length of rivers in the district is about 1,033 kilometers.

TABLE 2.4: District Khiri–Cropping Pattern

Major crops	Area Sown	
	Hectares	Percentage
Paddy	1,44,767	23.71
Wheat	1,73,045	28.34
Maize	21,890	3.59
Masoor	22,489	3.68
Sarson	21,658	3.55
Sugarcane	1,36,602	22.37
Barley	4120	0.67
Jowar	4169	0.68
Urad	6938	1.14
Gram	7357	1.20
Arhar	7536	1.23

Source : Statistical Bulletin–District Khiri,–1989 (Hindi Edition)

There is massive canal network of Sharda system in the district. Main canals comprising the Sitapur and Khiri Branches of the system flow in the district. Their distributories and further channels irrigate the vast plain area of the district. The total canal length in the district is

1,670 kilometers. The Sharda canal irrigation system and especially with the construction of feeder channels in the district pose serious problems in water resource management; salinization, waterlogging and alkalinization of soils. These problems are caused by irrigating soils with poor drainage, high water table and high evapo-transpiration rates. The productivity of vast area of agricultural lands in the Blocks of Nekah and Ramiabehd has been reduced and large areas of agricultural lands have gone to the category of non-agricultural uses. Due to heavy seepage, the usar areas, not suitable for agricultural crops, in the district have gone up from 4,451 hectares in 1969-70 to 9,816 hectares in 1987-88.

The district has got an average rainfall of 1,069 m.m. According to an estimate by the hydrologists, about 26 per cent of rainfall evaporates, 25 per cent is absorbed into soil and remaining 49 per cent is being used for irrigation purposes. For 1970-71, the estimates for groundwater in the district were established at about 11.39 lakh sq.ft. About one-fourth of this quantity was estimated to be available in only Nidhasan Tehsil. Attempts are being made to explore the maximum use of this groundwater. There are 719 government tubewells in the district. Quite a large number of boreholes are also being used for irrigation purposes by the farmers both with the electric operated pumps, diesel engines and animal power. The district has 206 wells, 36 persian wheels, 2,572 pump sets being used for lifting the surface water besides 58,378 pumps installed on bore holes and 13,298 private tubewells. This shows the high percentage of irrigated area to the total cropped area of the district. In large part of the district and especially in the Tarai area, due to high water table, crops like sugarcane and paddy are cultivated without irrigation, otherwise the water table is around at 3-8 meters and the usual depth of water for drinking and irrigation purposes is 20-30 feet. About 85 per cent of the area is irrigated by tubewells and remaining 15 per cent by canals in the district.

Forest Resources

Forest area in Lakhim Pur Khiri district accounts for over 163.75 thousand hectares, i.e. 21 per cent of the total reporting area. Almost all the forest area lies in the Tarai zone of the district. Proportionately, the district has more area under forests as compared to other districts of Uttar Pradesh. The per capita forest area in the district is 0.08 hectare. Tehsil Nidhasan has got about 30 per cent of its area under forests. Almost all the forest areas of the district are under reserve forests comprising Sal, Tun, Shisham species along with plantations of Tendu, Ghori, Asna, Khair and Haldu. The total forest area of the district can be divided according to the following major species:

Sal forests
Miscellaneous forests
Grass and bushes lands

The main categories of the forests in Khiri district fall under:

Tropical–Semi evergreen forests
Tropical–Moist deciduous forests
Littoral or Swamp forests
Tropical–dry deciduous forests

Geographical distribution of the forest area in Tarai region of Khiri district is well specified. The distribution pattern of the species available in the area could be located as :

1. *Forests in the surrounding of River Jorha*

Syzygium cuminii	(Jamun)
Ficus recemose	(Goolar)
Streblus asper	(Sihor)
Barringtonia acutangula	(Nyora)
Furn grasses	

2. *Sal forests of Damar River area*

Shorea robusta	(Sal)

Terminalia bellerica	(Behera)
Terminalia alata	(Asna)
Lagerstroemia parviflora	(Ghori)
Tectona grandis	(Sagon)
Adina cardifolia	(Haldu)
Mallotus phillipensis	(Rohni)

3. *Forests of Jalod Plain*

Shorea robusta	(Sal)
Kydia calycina	(Poola)
Adina cardifolia	(Haldu)
Lagerstroemia parviflora	(Ghori)
Terminalia alata	(Asna)

4. *Forests of Fanta Plain*

(a) Moist sal savannah forests:

Shorea robusta	(Sal)
Randia uliginosa	(Pinsar)
Acacia catechu	(Khair)
Adina cardifolia	(Haldu)
Dalbergia sissoo	(Shisham)
Bombex ceiba	(Samul)

(b) Swamp forests:

Bombex ceiba	(Samul)
Terminalia alata	(Asna)
Mallotus phillipensis	(Rohni)
Bombex ceiba	(Samul)
Shorea robusta	(Sal)
Acacia catechu	(Khair)
Syzygium cuminii	(Jamum)

5. *Forests in the surroundings of River Mohana*

Bombex ceiba	(Samul)
Adina cardifolia	(Haldoo)
Dalbergia sissoo	(Shisham)
Butea monosperma	(Dhak)

6. *Forests near Digma River*

Acacia catechu	(Khair)
Dalbergia sissoo	(Shisham)
Syzygium cuminii	(Jamum)

Forest Department in Khiri district maintains a number of nurseries in and outside the forest area. A massive programme of afforestation on vacant forest lands is a permanent feature of the department. The prominent species most suitable to local conditions under the department are being planted. Some of these species; *Acacia catechu, Dalbergia sissoo, Adina cardifolia, Bombex ceiba, Tectona grandis, Cedrela toona, Albizia lebbeck, Shorea robusta* and *eucalyptus* have been planted on Fanta and other open lands in the forest zone. The hybrid *eucalyptus* for the first time in the forest area was planted in 1962. Its plantation was carried out on annual basis till 1977 and since then no *eucalyptus* tree has been planted on the reserve forest land of the district.

Afforestation programme is also being undertaken on LMC lands, alongwith railway lines, canal sides and road sides by the Forest Department. The nurseries developed by the Forest Department outside the forest zone provide saplings to the farmers. Emphasis is being given on species most suitable to fuelwood under the programme. The saplings distributed to the villagers under the social forestry programme account for about 3.50 lakh during 1989-90.

Livestock and Grazing Resources

The district Khiri, according to 1987 livestock census has about 1,415,590 heads of livestock. The distribution of total livestock population is as follows:

TABLE 2.5: District Khiri–Livestock Population–1987

Categories	Number	Percentage to total
Cows	508,751	35.94
Buffaloes	359,377	25.39
Sheep	18,959	1.34
Goats	269,992	19.07
Pony and Horses	2,780	0.20
Pigs	30,486	2.15
Donkeys, Mules	216,672	15.31
Total	1,415,590	100.00

Source : Statistical Bulletin–District Khiri, 1989 (Hindi Edition)

According to land utilization data for the Khiri district,

the total grazing land area is only 1,277 hectares. Considering the availability of grazing lands which are about two per cent of the total reporting area, the livestock density per hectare is very high. The livestock population on 100 hectares of the reporting area comes to 183 and per 1,000 persons it is 725. The number of milching animals per 100 persons comes to about 15.

Considering the two figures–livestock population and grazing lands–the area per head of livestock works out to be very negligible. As a matter of fact, in the intensive cultivated cropped area, the grazing practice is not common and leaving apart the forest zone most of the district fell under this category. Livestock in this condition are raised on cattle sheds and on chaffed fodder. Herding is not common, neither the villagers have too many livestock nor there are sufficient vacant lands for grazing in the rural surroundings of Khiri district. Keeping cattle for milk purposes is also not very popular especially among the large and well-to-do farmers. This characteristic is entirely different than the farmers of the same strata in western Uttar Pradesh, who usually raise the milk cattle both for household requirements and to sell the milk in the market.

The district Khiri has 10 forest villages predominated by Tharu tribe. Tharu people have facility to graze their livestock in the forest area. But the number of livestock and their population is a fraction of the district data and thus have little impact on either programme.

Milk production and productivity is very low in the district. The local bred cows of 'Kharigarh' hardly yields one litre of milk and in most of the cases it is less than a litre.

Buffaloes are also of poor breed with small quantity of milk production per animal. Although the number of livestock in the district, due to large area under forests, is higher, the milk production and productivity per animal seems to be the lowest in the region.

In the absence of grazing practices, the livestock are raised on wheat straw, jowar, green fodder like berseem and lucerne, sugarcane tops and occasionally on paddy straw. Before supplying to the cattle, these fodder are chaffed and as case may be mixed with concentrates etc.

3

REQUIREMENT AND SUPPLY OF FUELWOOD AT THE HOUSEHOLD LEVEL

From time immomerial to the present day, fuelwood has been extensively used in almost every human community as a fuel for cooking, heating and lighting. Even in the modern times where other commercial fuels have been developed, the fuelwood is used by over seventy per cent of the world's human population as domestic fuel. Majority of these people live in the developing world. During the last two-three decades, the pressure of population growth and the commercial exploitation of timber resources in less developed countries have made fuelwood increasingly scarce.

In India, during this period, growing concern has been expressed over the massive scale of deforestation which is occurring almost in all parts of the country. It may be safely assumed that in majority of the cases/areas the principal cause of deforestation is the growing demand for fuelwood. The development and harnessing of other sources of energy to augment or replace fuelwood in the rural areas has been successful in a very limited way. For example, bio-gas, solar cookers and high technology options such as photovoltaics etc, have not been as widely adopted as was originally thought. Many problems have been and are being faced to make them popular in the rural masses. More and more, it is recognised that fuelwood alongwith agricultural/animal wastes in some of the parts of the country are likely to remain as the major domestic fuel in the households, at least in the forseeable future. Increasing the supply of fuelwood, is possible through re-afforestation programmes on degraded lands but experiences have shown many difficulties in the way to persuade the people to grow trees on these lands.[1]

In view of the sudden rise in world oil prices in the early 'seventies besides the acute shortage of fuelwood, worldwide attention was paid for the development and dissemination of improved *Chulhas* for cooking as an immediate way of relieving the crisis. The traditional methods of cooking on an open fire or a simple mud hearth were regarded as being very inefficient for energy saving. Many versions of the improved *Chulhas* were developed. These are being used by the rural community but again with not very much satisfaction. The acceptance has been there but within a very limited society. Thus the objective that the reduction of the demand for fuelwood would be effected by this programme has dim prospects.

The following analysis based on the empirical evidence calculates the domestic demand and local supply of fuelwood in the two sets of data collected from Hills and Tarai areas of the State of Uttar Pradesh.

The total domestic energy requirement in the villages under study comes to about 34,252.249 MJ per household in Pauri district and about 41,852.632 MJ in Khiri district. Then the per capita requirement per annum comes to 5,241.97 MJ in Pauri and 4,999.75 MJ in Khiri district respectively.

The major contribution to this total domestic energy in the households has been fuelwood, dung cakes, agricultural/crop residues, kerosene oil, etc. Use of LPG, bio-gas and electricity are not very common means of energy supply in the kitchen in the rural community under investigations. Out of the total 260 investigated households, only one has reported the use of bio-gas during the rainy season in Rukandi Pur village (Tarai area), another household in Hills area (Pauri district) has reported the use of electricity occasionally for cooking purposes and two households also in Hills villages have reported the use of LPG. Thus four households use these sources of energy besides other most common sources of energy supply i.e., non-conventional, in the studied area

(Fig. 3.1). The total consumption of the fuel in the studied households is given in the following table:

TABLE 3.1: Total Domestic use of Fuel in the Studied Villages

Type of Fuel		Hills	Tarai
I. **Non-conventional**			
Dung Cake	(kg)	52,659	118,680
Fuelwood	(kg)	218,097	365,235
Agricultural Residues	(kg)	—	125,820
Bio-gas	(hrs.)	---	30
II. **Conventional**			
Electricity	(Units)	135	—
Coke	(kg)	—	660
Kerosene oil	(Lts)	7,452	2,850
LPG	(kg)	216	—

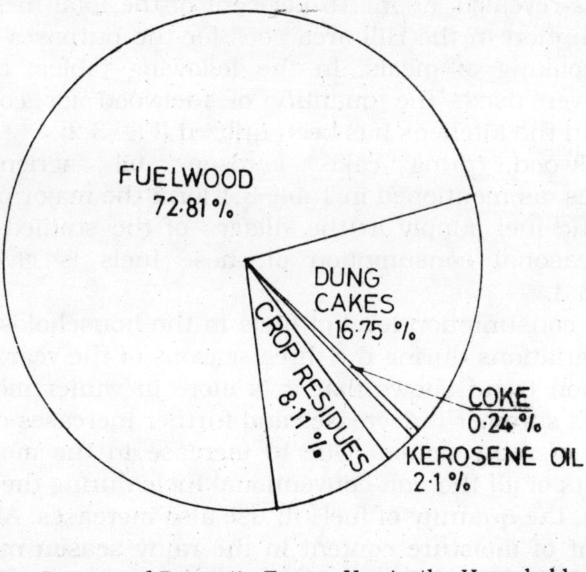

FIG. 3.1: **Sources of Domestic Energy Use in the Households in Tarai Area**

The fuelwood consumption in the households has been mainly for kitchens and especially for cooking of foods. But in Hill areas, the heating of water and warming of houses during the prolonged winter season have also been the major consumer of this source of fuel supply. In the Tarai areas only food cooking is reported with the fuel-wood. Table 3.2 shows the fuelwood utilization in Hill areas.

TABLE 3.2: Consumption of Fuelwood in the Hill areas

Purpose	Annual use of fuelwood	
	Kgs.	Percentages
Cooking	184,287	84.50
Water heating	24,490	11.23
House warming	9,320	4.27
Total use	218,097	100.00

As is revealed, about 15 per cent of the total fuelwood consumption in the Hill area goes for the purposes other than cooking of meals. In the following tables, except whereever used, the quantity of fuelwood for cooking meals in the kitchens has been utilized (Fig. 3.2).

Fuelwood, dung cake, kerosene oil, agricultural residues, as mentioned in Table 3.1 form the major part of domestic fuel supply in the villages of the studied area. The seasonal consumption of these fuels is given in Table 3.3.

The consumption level of fuels in the households have wide variations during the three seasons of the year. Consumption trend shows that it is more in winter months, towards summer it decreases and further increases on the arrival of rainy period. Due to increase in the moisture contents of all the non-conventional fuels during the rainy season, the quantity of fuels in use also increases. Also on account of moisture content in the rainy season most of these fuels, are left unburnt and thrown away by the users. Both these aspects have increased the quantity of

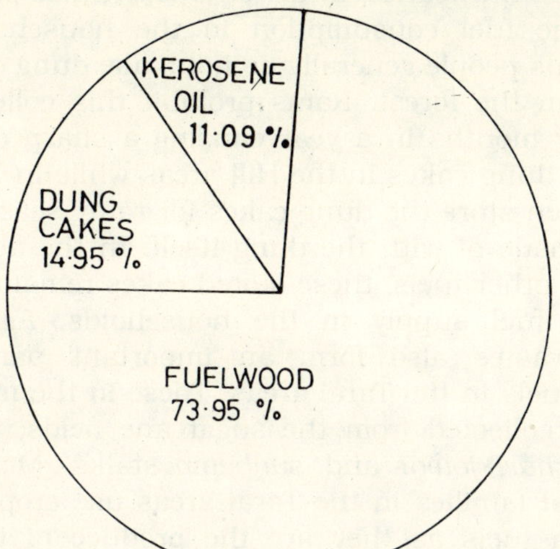

FIG. 3.2: Sources of Domestic Energy Use in Households in the Hills

TABLE 3.3: Seasonal Consumption of Major Fuels in the Reporting Households

Fuel/seasons	Seasonal Consumption of Fuel in each Reporting Household					
	Winter		Summer		Rainy	
	Households	Units	Households	Units	Households	Units
Dung cakes (kg)						
(i) Hills	89	315	89	270	10	48
(ii) Tarai	125	327	125	255	123	372
Fuelwood (kg)						
(i) Hills	90	657	90	558	90	831
(ii) Tarai	165	756	165	606	165	852
Agricultural Residues (kg)						
(i) Hills	—	—	—	—	—	—
(ii) Tarai	103	429	100	381	92	471
Coke (kg)						
(i) Hills	—	—	—	—	—	—
(ii) Tarai	2	90	2	126	2	111
Kerosene oil (lts)						
(i) Hills	86	25.5	86	240	86	36.6
(ii) Tarai	91	18.9	27	20.4	27	20.4

fuels in the use in the rainy season. The prolonged winter season in both the areas under study have also positive effect on the fuel consumption in the households. The mountanous people generally do not make dung cakes but gather from the forest. Rains prohibit this collection for about four months in a year causing a sharp decline in the use of dung cakes in the Hill areas while in Tarai belt rural women store the dung cakes for rainy season in the storages made of with the dung itself. In the absence or scarcity of other fuels, these stored cakes remain the only source of fuel supply in the households. Agricultural residues/wastes also form an important part of the domestic fuels in the Tarai areas. These in the majority of cases are collected from the sugarcane fields, and form part of *arhar, jowar* and *sunhemp* stalks. Most of the agricultural families in the Tarai areas use crop residues as kitchen fuels as they are the produce of their own fields. Crop residues and dung cakes in the area under study are never marketed. In rare cases, the poorest strata of the society sometimes exchange these fuels within their own groups. In the rural surrounding of Hills, fuelwood is never sold except by those people who earn their livelihood through this activity. The family collections of fuelwood in the Hills are generally meant for domestic use. The per capita use of major fuels for domestic purposes is given in Table 3.4.

TABLE 3.4: Per Capita Annual use of Different Fuels in the Household

Main domestic fuels		Hills	Tarai
Dung cakes	(kg)	89.55	87.99
Fuelwood	(kg)	313.41	270.75
Crop residues	(kg)	—	33.15
Coke	(kg)	—	0.48
Kerosene oil	(Lts)	12.66	2.10

As is evident from the above table that the use of dung cakes per person in the two studied areas are at the same level; fuelwood and kerosene oil are more consumed in

Hills while crop residues and coke are in use in the Tarai areas. Dung cakes are a recent introduction in the Hills and even now a good number of villagers do not use it as a source of domestic energy. The use of dung cakes for fuel is a problem of wide concern but it is more relevant to the Hill villages because compost is the only source of manure for agriculture in most part of the Pauri district and thus its use as fuel has adverse effect on agricultural productivity. A comparatively high value of dung cake use in the Hill areas is due to the fact that majority of the households use *Angithi* for cooking the night meals. This *Angithi* is generally fed by dung cakes and besides cooking keeps the houses warm during the winter nights – a long time practice adopted by the villagers. The total energy consumption in the studied areas is given in Table 3.5.

TABLE 3.5: The Per Capita Total Energy Consumption for the Domestic Purposes

Source of energy supply	Total energy use (MJ)	
	Hills	Tarai
Dung	783.89 (14.95)	770.24 (16.75)
Fuelwood	3,876.55 (73.95)	3,348.89 (72.81)
Crop residues	– –	373.13 (8.11)
Coke	– –	11.03 (0.24)
Kerosene oil	581.53 (11.09)	96.46 (2.10)
Total Per annum	5,241.97 (100.00)	4,599.75 (100.00)
Total per day	14.36	12.60

Note: Figures in parentheses show percentages to total energy consumption.

The figures of the above table reveal that the total annual domestic energy consumption of the households is about 5,242 MJ per capita in the Hills and 4,600 MJ in the Tarai belt. On the basis of these calculations, the per capita per day use of energy for domestic purposes comes to 14.36 MJ and 12.60 MJ for the two areas respectively (Fig. 3.3).

In Hill areas, the utilization of domestic energy is about 14 per cent higher as compared to Tarai areas. This is mainly due to the prolonged nature of cold winter season in the mountainous terrain of the area. The table also reveals that a little less than three-fourths of the total energy is constituted by the fuelwood in both areas under investigation. Thus fuelwood is the major source of contribution to the total energy supply for domestic purposes in the households. Considering this, in the following paragraphs emphasis will be given to the supply and development of fuelwood in the study areas. The frequency distribution of households as seen with total use of fuelwood is given in Table 3.6.

TABLE 3.6: Distribution of Households According to the Annual Fuelwood Use

Level of Fuelwood Use (kg)	Hills		Tarai	
	Households	Percentage	Households	Percentage
Upto 500	2	2.2	7	4.1
501-1,000	1	1.1	10	5.9
1,001-1,500	3	3.3	30	17.6
1,501-2,000	17	18.9	38	22.4
2,001-2,500	18	20.0	13	7.6
2,501-3,000	25	27.8	30	17.6
3,001-Above	24	26.7	42	24.7
Total	90	100.00	170	100.0

The results of the above table show that the majority of households (66 per cent) in the Hills fall in the fuelwood consumption level of 1,501-3,000 kgs per annum. In the Tarai belt, 40 per cent households are located within the range of 1,001-2,000 kgs per annum. Quite a large number of households (one-fourth) have their annual consumption of fuelwood over 3,000 kgs in both the areas separately (Fig. 3.4).

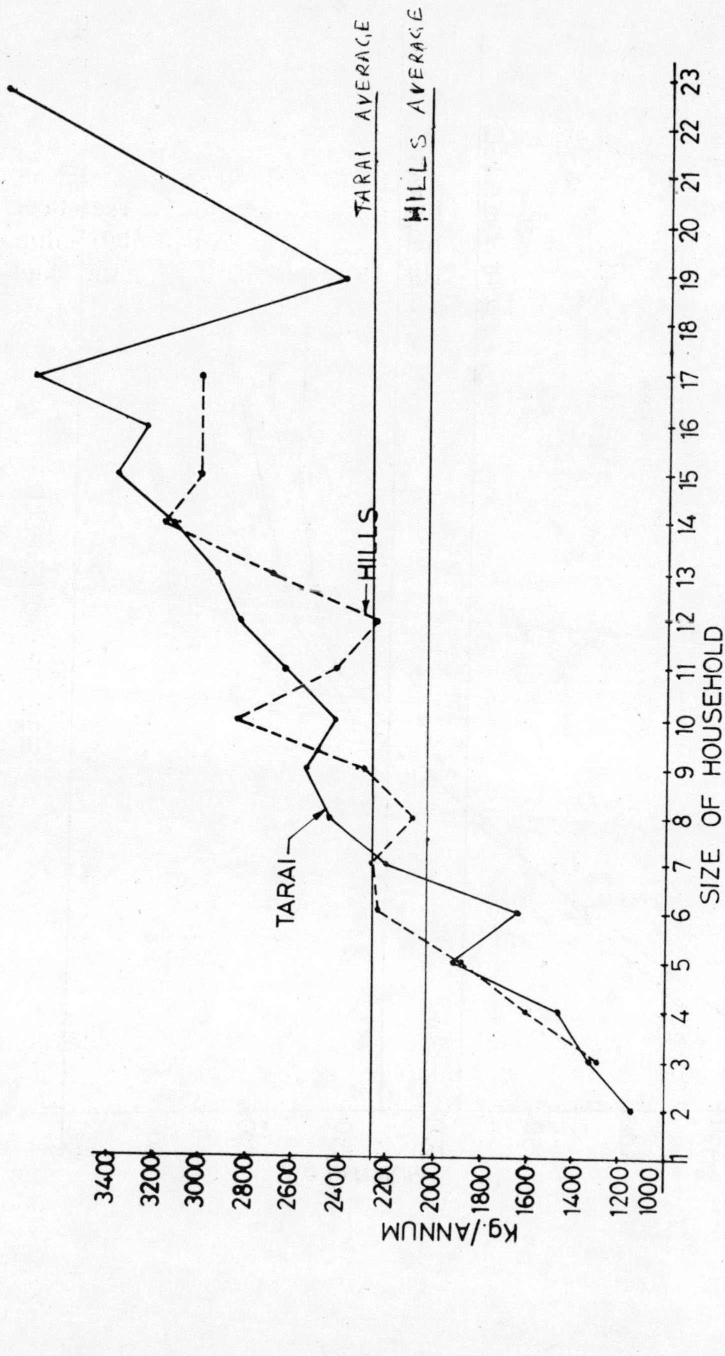

FIG. 3.3: Use of Fuelwood in the Household

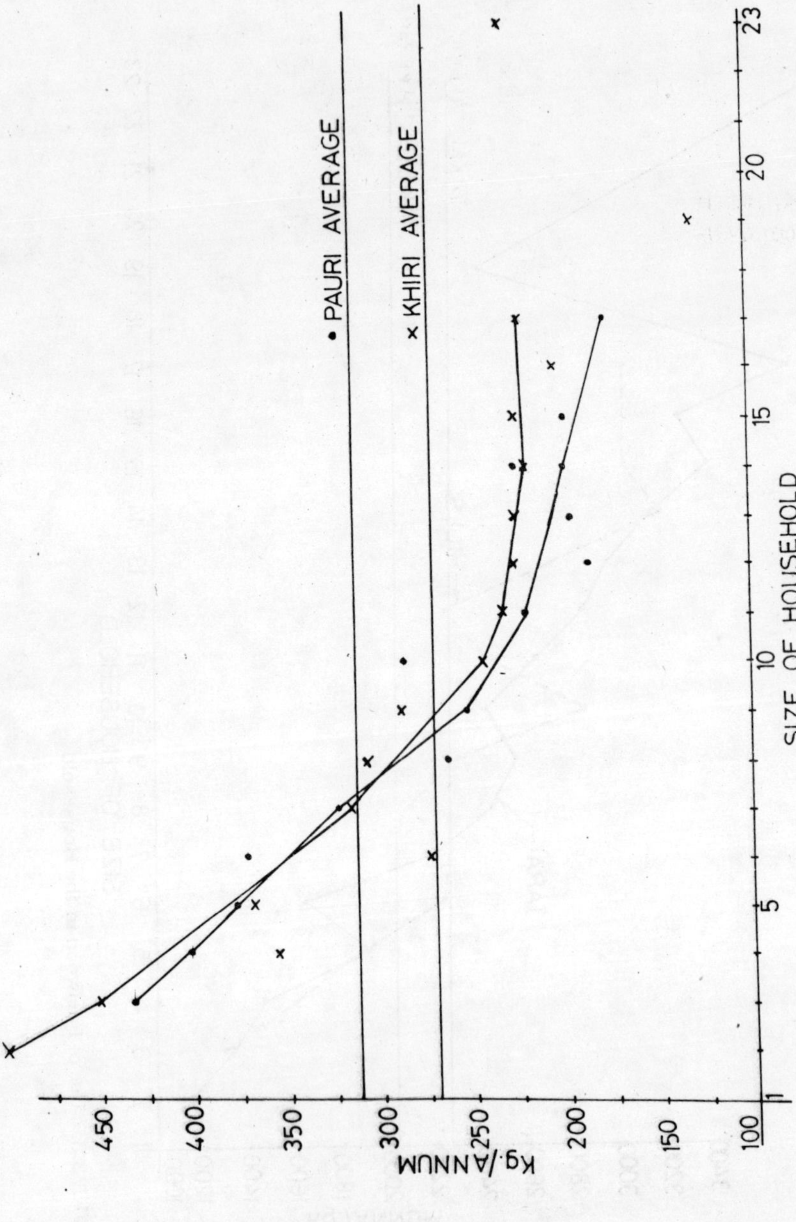

FIG. 3.4: Per Capita Fuelwood Consumption

Tables 3.7 and 3.8 show the per household and per capita consumption of fuelwood in the households according to their size. As is evident, the per household requirement of fuelwood increases as the size of family increases but the per capita use has got a reverse position, i.e., with the increase the size of household the per capita consumption of fuelwood decreases. Smallest the size of the household greater the consumption of fuelwood and *vice versa.*

TABLE 3.7: Per Household Use of the Fuelwood for Domestic Purposes (kg)

Size of Household	Hills	Tarai
2	–	1,171.87
3	1,304.25	1,354.69
4	1,602.30	1,442.31
5	1,885.38	1,857.75
6	2,235.00	1,638.46
7	2,241.43	2,200.00
8	2,100.00	2,460.94
9	2,275.00	2,579.17
10	2,850.00	2,425.00
11	2,415.00	2,626.87
12	2,250.00	2,828.57
13	2,700.00	2,925.00
14	3,150.0	3,120.00
15	3,000.00	3,375.00
16	–	3,225.00
17	3,000.00	3,795.00
19	–	2,400.00
23	–	5,250.00
Mean	2,047.6333	2,213.5455
Std.Dev.	603.2074	882.2211
Variance	363,859.1112	778,314.0299
N	90	170

Besides the size of the household, the per capita consumption of fuelwood has also been influenced by a number of factors, e.g. seasonal weather pattern, utensils used for cooking, type and quality of *chulha* and quality of wood used for cooking. Table 3.9 shows these parameters in practice in the areas of study.

TABLE 3.8: Per Capita Use of Fuelwood for Domestic Purposes (kg)

Size of Household	Hills	Tarai
2	—	581.94
3	434.75	451.59
4	400.58	360.58
5	377.08	371.55
6	372.50	273.08
7	320.20	314.29
8	262.50	307.62
9	252.78	286.57
10	285.00	242.50
11	219.55	238.81
12	187.50	235.71
13	207.69	225.00
14	225.00	222.86
15	200.00	225.00
16	—	201.56
17	176.47	223.24
19	—	126.32
23	—	228.26
Average	313.41	270.75

TABLE 3.9: Percentage of Households in Use of Different Cooking Practices

Pattern of cooking	Percentage of households	
	Hills	Tarai
Use of cooking appliances		
Open *chulha*	98.89	97.06
Improved *chulha*	2.22	2.94
Sigri/Angithi	86.67	20.59
Use of cooking Utensils:		
Clay pots	2.22	6.47
Aluminium pots	97.78	98.24
Pressure cookers	97.78	35.88

In the rural surrounding of the studied area, it is clear that almost all households use open *chulha* for cooking their meals. The use of portable *chulha* (*sigri*) is very common in the Hills (87 per cent households) while only one-fifth of the households use *sigri* in the Tarai areas. Aluminium pots are generally used for cooking in both the districts. The use of pressure cooker is more common in the Hill areas as compared to the Tarai belt.

The place of fuelwood in the cooking of different meals and type of wood in use in the studied areas is given in Table 3.10.

TABLE 3.10: Use of Fuelwood in Cooking and its Type as Reported by the Households

Fuelwood	Percentage of reported households	
	Hills	Tarai
Fuelwood being used for the preparation of:		
Breakfast	95.56	58.82
Noon meals	98.89	94.12
Evening meals	98.89	97.65
Tea and snacks	85.56	10.00
Quality of fuelwood used:		
Dry wood*	97.78	97.65
Dry + wet	92.22	97.06

* Air dry wood.

The above table clearly shows that fuelwood is extensively used by the rural people for all the meal cookings in the Hill areas. In Tarai also, except breakfast and tea preparations, fuelwood is the main source of fuel supply for food cookings.

The type of fuelwood used in the rural households varies from logs to branches/twigs, leaves and sometimes barks. Lopping of branches is very common especially for Bhimal (*Grewia oppositifolia*) in the Hill areas and for Babul (*Acacia spps.*) and Shisham (*Dalbergia sissoo*) in the Tarai areas. Otherwise mainly dead trees are collected either from forests or from village common lands. Table 3.11 shows different types of fuelwoods used in the households.

TABLE 3.11: Type of Fuelwood Used for the Domestic Requirements

Type of fuelwood	Percentage of households	
	Hills	Tarai
Logs	11.11	–
Branches/Twigs	93.33	96.46
Dead trees	95.56	97.07
Barks	–	0.59
Leaves	–	2.35

Logs are not used as fuelwood in the Tarai belt but eleven per cent households in the Hill areas reported that they have used them as domestic fuel. Twigs/branches and that of the dead trees mainly form the major supply of fuel in the households. Ninety-three per cent households in Hills and 96 per cent households in Tarai use twigs. Cutting live trees is not reported in both the areas under investigation. Tree barks and leaves also formed part of the fuel supply in a few of the households in the Tarai belt. Species used as fuel and the respective number of households in use have been given in the Table 3.12.

Except *eucalyptus* which has been recently adopted as fuelwood in the households, all the other species have long been used in both the areas under investigation. Especially pinus in the Hills and *shisham* in the Tarai areas form the major part of domestic fuels which are easily available in the interior side of the rural areas. *Acacia spps.* are plentiful in the plains/tarai and *toons* and *quercus* have sufficient plantations in the Hills. Mango as a fuelwood is also being used by a number of households in the Tarai areas.

The social/farm forestry programmes in the areas under study were introduced during the early 'eighties. By the time the field investigations of the present study were being conducted it was expected that the plantations raised in those years would have reached their life of about 8-9 years i.e., they might be in a position to produce sufficient biomass for domestic fuel supply. Considering this idea, data were collected to have a comparative study of the two periods, i.e., around 1982-83 and 1991-92.

TABLE 3.12: **Species used as Fuel in the Households**

Areas/Species	Reporting Households (Percentage)
Hills:	
Pinus longifolia	95.6
Cedrela toona	87.8
Quercus incana	86.3
Grewia oppositifolia	55.9
Tarai:	
Eucalyptus	95.0
Dalbergia sissoo	94.5
Acacia nilotica/Acacia catechu	93.3
Azadirachta indica	31.30
Mangifera indica	17.20

Results of the data analysis represent a very interesting findings. The results show that although there has been no change during the period in the type of fuelwood used for domestic purposes and the same pattern followed for the use of twigs/branches as main sources of supply in majority of the households, a marked difference is, however, noticed in other aspects of fuelwood supply, i.e., in the sources of supplies, dependence ratios, distance of fuelwood collection, etc. Table 3.13 shows the details regarding the above results.

There has been a marked increase in the number of households in the Hill areas who use fuelwood from their own production resources. Their number has gone up from 46 to 86 i,e., over 46 per cent increase during the last ten-year period. Besides increase in the number of households, they have reported that own farm production supply of fuelwood has also increased in the household. Presently, they have been using fuelwood from their own field production for about 3.5 months in a year as against 2.6 months before the start of the social/farm forestry programme in the area. The dependence for fuelwood on forests has decreased from 4.2 months to 3.1 months in a year.

TABLE 3.13: Dependence of Different Sources of Fuelwood Supply in the Households

Source of fuelwood supply	Early eighties		1991-92	
	Reporting House-holds	Months in the year	Reporting House-holds	Months in the year
Hills				
Own field produce	46	2.6	86	3.5
Forest collections	90	4.2	90	3.1
Community land collections	89	5.6	89	5.8
Tarai				
Own field produce	61	3.2	61	4.7
Forest collections	40	3.4	40	3.6
Community land collections	136	3.3	136	4.0
Road/canal/railway/ side collections	106	3.7	105	3.6
Purchases	105	6.5	101	5.2

In the Tarai area, two marked instances have been reported in the dependency period. Own field supplies have increased from 3.2 months to 4.7 months in a year while dependence on purchased supplies shows a negative effect i.e., from 6.5 months to 5.2 months in a year (Fig. 3.5).

Table 3.14 shows the total fuelwood supply by different sources in the villages.

Fuelwood produced on the growers fields contribute over 16 per cent of the total supply of domestic fuels both in the Hills and Tarai belt. The trees in the Tarai area are generally grown both on the boundaries of the plots and in a number of cases under the block plantations. In the Hills, the trees are scattered and spread all over the plots area. Fuelwood collected from forests accounts for 21 per cent in the Hills and 7 per cent in Tarai to the total supply. The major source of domestic fuel supply is, however, the community lands which provide 63 per cent to total in the Hills and 29 per cent in the Tarai belt. Other main sources of fuelwood supplies in the Tarai areas are roadside collections (15 per cent), purchases from markets (12 per cent) and purchases from villages (14 per cent). Besides small quantities are collected from canal sides, railway line side and from other farms (Fig. 3.6).

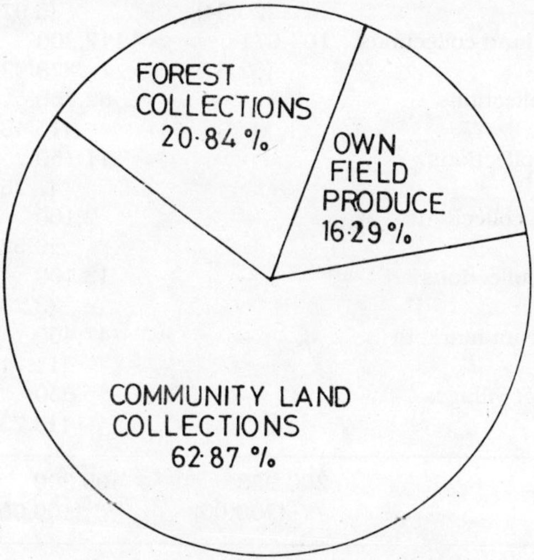

FIG. 3.5: Sources of Fuelwood Supply in Hill Areas

Thus according to the figures of the above table it could easily be concluded that the households are more dependent on the collected fuelwoods (except for about one-fourth availability in the Tarai areas which is purchased against cash payments) and these collections contribute to about 84 per cent in the Hills and 58 per cent in the Tarai areas of the total domestic supplies. Though the situation is changing and the social/farm forestry programmes have started showing their results, it will take a long time for farmers/landholders to become self-sufficient in their domestic energy needs. The large proportion of rural population, without land, has always to be dependent on the local collections from various sources as mentioned in Fig. 3.7.

TABLE 3.14: Total Fuelwood Supply by Different Sources in the Villages (kgs)

Source of fuelwood supply	Hills	Tarai
Own field produce	42,512 (16.29)	67,650 (16.69)
Forest collections	54,370 (20.84)	28,250 (6.97)
Community land collections	164,071 (62.87)	117,200 (28.92)
Road side collections	—	62,750 (15.48)
Canal side collections	—	11,150 (2.75)
Railway side collections	—	2,100 (0.52)
Other farm collections	—	13,100 (3.23)
Purchased from markets	—	47,450 (11.71)
Purchased for villages	—	55,650 (13.73)
Total	260,953 (100.00)	405,300 (100.00)

Note: Figures in parentheses show percentage to total supply.

The change in the fuelwood supply during the reference period and decade prior to that is given in Table 3.15.

The massive plantations process that had taken place during the years of the 'eighties have started showing its impact on the fuelwood supply in the households both from individual plantations as well as from community plantations. In the Hill areas, the fuelwood supply from own plantations have increased over eight per cent during this period. The impact has been more impressive in the Tarai areas and that accounts for about 59 per cent increase through own field supplies. Dependence on forest supplies has come down in the Hills while it has shown an increase of 12 per cent in the Tarai belt. Fuelwood collections from community lands have increased in both the districts.

TABLE 3.15: Changes in the Fuelwood Collections Used for Domestic Purposes (kgs/household)

Source of fuelwood supply	Early Eighties kgs/household	1991-92 kgs/household	Percentage change
Hills			
Own field produce	463.33 (45)	500.14 (85)	+8.38
Forest collections	822.47 (89)	604.11 (90)	-26.55
Community land collections	1,641.66 (90)	1,823.01 (90)	+11.05
Tarai			
Own field produce	698.68 (61)	1,109.1 (61)	+58.73
Forest collections	700.00 (36)	784.72 (36)	+12.10
Community land collections	665.60 (141)	837.14 (140)	+25.77
Road side collections	514.01 (107)	597.61 (105)	+16.26
Canal side collections	442.85 (28)	484.78 (23)	+9.47
Railway line collections	337.50 (8)	350.00 (6)	+3.70
Other farms collections	519.23 (26)	503.84 (26)	-2.96
Purchases from markets	1,304.00 (50)	968.36 (49)	-25.74
Purchases from villages	1,269.23 (650)	883.33 (63)	-30.40

Note: Figures in parentheses show the number of reporting households.

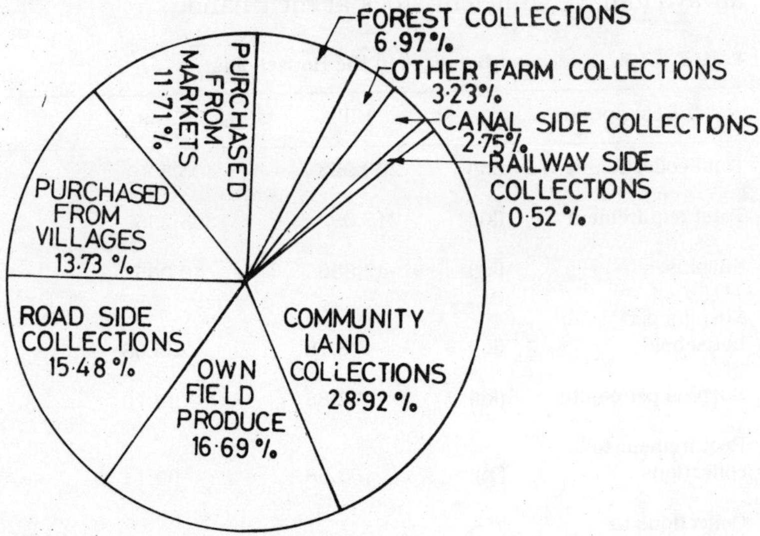

FIG. 3.6: Sources of Fuelwood Supply in Tarai Areas

The fuelwood collected by three sources in Tarai areas which are unreported in the Hills has shown an increase of 3 per cent from railway line sides to about 16 per cent from roadsides in the decades. The fuelwood collection from other farmers fields in the Tarai areas has come down by 3 per cent. A remarkable down fall of fuelwood supplies through purchases in the Tarai areas has been observed. This is about 26 per cent in purchases from markets and over 30 per cent from other villages. The fuelwood balance based on the households information is given in Table 3.16.

The selected villages under Hill areas are surrounded by good forest cover both protected and civil. Thus there is adequate fuelwood supply in the nearby areas. Rural people illegally collect the fuelwood and wood deficit is not reported. Surpluses to the utilization are observed at the household level. This may be partly because the rural people have a habit to stock sufficient quantities of fuel and partly because it being collected free is sometimes over collected. And also because the fuelwood collection is a females task they are more conscious about its use, i.e., always to have sufficient stock at their hand.

TABLE 3.16: Fuelwood Balances in the Households

Description		Hills	Tarai
Total collections	(kg)	260,953	405,300
Total requirement	(kg)	218,097	365,235
Surpluses	(kg)	42,856	40,065
Surplus per household	(kg)	478.18	235.68
Surplus per capita	(kg)	72.88	29.70
Requirement to collections	(%)	83.58	90.11
Collections to requirement	(%)	119.65	110.97

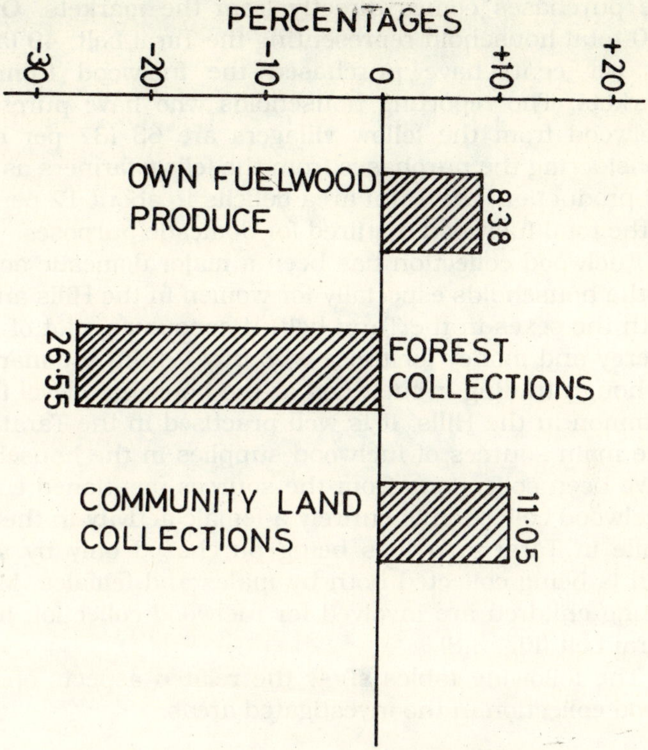

FIG. 3.7: **Percentage Change in Fuelwood Supply During the Last Decade (Hill Areas)**

The situation in the Tarai belt is different. Rural people over there stock fuelwood as a buffer stock. Their priority remains to consume the crop residues first and then dung cakes. They try as far as possible to stock the fuelwood. Dung cakes and crop residues in the Tarai area are not stocked on a large scale. A few of the residents reported the stock of dung cakes for the rainy season. Tarai belt is a wood deficit area where about one-fourth fuelwood is purchased by the consumer households. Many of the farmers have planted trees of fuelwood for self-consumption. This is being the perception of the people that their own farm production of fuelwood exceeded their requirement and farmers/growers have sold off its large quantity to the fellow villagers. The remaining quantity of the purchases comes directly from the markets. Of the 170 total household representing the Tarai belt, 49 (about 29 per cent) have purchased the fuelwood from the markets. The reporting households who have purchased fuelwood from the fellow villagers are 63 (37 per cent). Considering the purchases from the fellow farmers as a local production, the Tarai area deficits to about 12 per cent of the total fuelwood required for domestic purposes.

Fuelwood collection has been a major domestic activity in the households especially for women in the Hills and for both the sexes in the Tarai belt. It consumes a lot of time, energy and money for those who buy it from the markets. Although trading in fuelwood at the household level is not common in the Hills, it is well practised in the Tarai belt. The main sources of fuelwood supplies in the households have been collections from the sources mentioned earlier. Fuelwood collection is entirely a female activity in the Hills while in Tarai area it is being purchased only by males and is being collected both by males and females. Mostly young children are involved for fuelwood collection in the Tarai belt (Fig. 3.8).

The following tables show the related aspects on fuelwood collection in the investigated areas.

TABLE 3.17: Fuelwood Collected* by Males in the Tarai Area

Description	Participating Households	Units
Average distance of fuelwood-collection from the village (kms)	158	4.43
Time spent on fuelwood collection in a single trip (hrs)	158	4.67
Quantity collected per trip (kgs)	158	66.37

* This included the quantity, distance and time spent on fuelwood purchases from the markets.

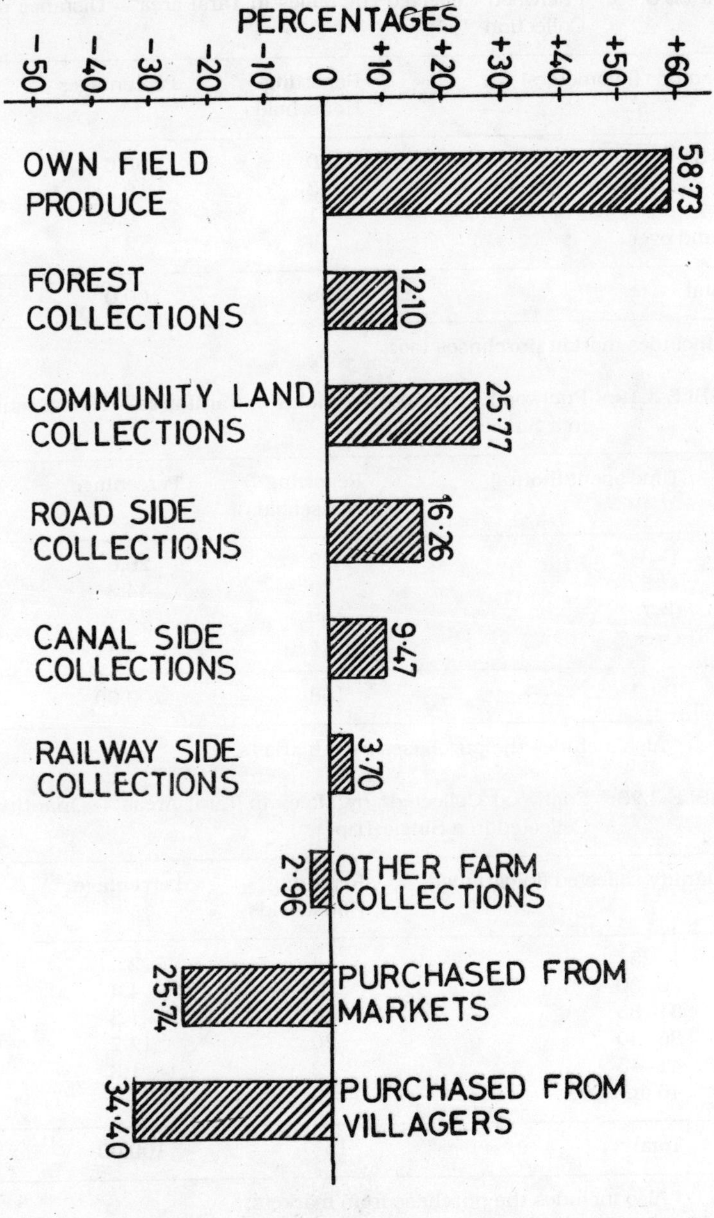

FIG. 3.8: Percentage Change in Fuelwood Supply During the Last Decade (Tarai Areas)

TABLE 3.18: Fuelwood Collected* by Males in Tarai area – Distance of Collection

Distance (kilometers)	Reporting Households	Percentages
1–3	140	88.6
4–5	13	8.2
6–7	1	0.6
8 and over	4	2.5
Total	158	100.0

* Includes market purchases too.

TABLE 3.19: Fuelwood Collected* by Males in Tarai area– Time Spent in a Single Collection

Time spent (hours)	Reporting Households	Percentage
1–3	42	26.6
4–5	70	44.3
6–7	39	24.7
Over 7	7	4.4
Total	158	100.00

* Also includes the purchases from markets.

TABLE 3.20: Fuelwood Collected* by Males in Tarai Areas – Quantity Collected in a Single Trip

Quantity collected (kilograms)	Reporting Households	Percentage
1–25	4	2.5
26–30	7	4.4
31–35	2	1.3
36–40	20	12.7
41–45	2	1.3
46 and Over	123	77.8
Total	158	100.00

* Also includes the purchase from markets.

TABLE 3.21: Fuelwood Collected by Females in the Hill Areas

Description	Participating Households	Units
Average distance of fuelwood collection from the village (kms)	90	2.1
Time spent on fuelwood collection in a single trip (hrs)	90	5.0
Quantity collected per trip (kgs)	90	33.52

TABLE 3.22: Fuelwood Collected by Females in Hill Areas – Distance of Collection

Distance (kilometers)	Reporting Households	Percentage
1–3	78	86.7
4–5	12	13.3
6–7	–	–
8 and over	–	–
Total	90	100.0

TABLE 3.23: Fuelwood Collected by Females in Hill Areas – Time Spent in a Single Collection

Time spent (hours)	Reporting Households	Percentage
1–3	–	
4–5	59	65.6
6–7	26	28.9
8 and over	5	5.6
Total	90	100.0

TABLE 3.24: Fuelwood Collected by Females in Hill Areas – Quantity Collected in a Single Trip

Quantity collected (Kilograms)	Reporting Households	Percentage
1–25	8	8.9
26–30	40	44.4
31–35	19	21.1
36–40	16	17.8
41–45	6	6.7
46 and over	1	1.1
Total	90	100.0

The result of the above tables summarises the distance of fuelwood collection by males and females from their village, the time spent in fuelwood collection and the quantity of the fuelwood collected. Of the total, about 95 per cent, i.e., 158 reporting respondents in the Tarai belt have provided the data . The average distance covered is 4.43 kms. per collection/trip and majority of the respondents (88 per cent) travel between one and three kilometers to collect fuelwood. Accordingly, they spent about 4.67 hours in the collection of fuelwood and 44 per cent of them, representing the majority, spent between 4 and 5 hours per trip. The fuelwood collected per trip comes to about 66 kilograms (including the purchases from markets) with over three-fourths of the respondents in a range of over 46 kgs and more in a single trip.

All the 90 investigated households in the Hills have reported that the collection of fuelwood was for domestic purposes. The average distance covered to collect the fuelwood, is about 2 kilometers and 87 households reported that they travel in a range up to 1-3 kms per trip. On an average the collection takes about 5 hours per trip and 66 per cent households collect between 4 and 5 hours. The quantity collected per trip comes to about 33 kgs, and majority, about 44 per cent of the households, reported the collected quantity in between 26–30 kgs.

NOTE

1. R.D. Sharma, *Economics of Fuelwood Production in Wastelands*, Concept Publishing Company, New Delhi, 1992.

4

IMPACT ON THE LIFE OF RURAL PEOPLE

Land reclamation and tree plantations have been the main activities for the improvement of eco-systems on the wasted lands in the two districts under study. In most of the cases, the land development programmes on wasted areas have been taken up at the individual level and without any financial assistance from outside. The only meagre assistance has reportedly been in the form of subsidy on saplings etc. purchased from the government nurseries. Most of the beneficiarics have indicated the indirect benefits they have received especially for the collection of fuelwoods, fodder and other materials from the lands so developed by the governmental agencies either on government or on community lands. The data collected have indicated that the normal life to some extent has become easy after the introduction of plantations programme on the wastelands. Although the gains to be observed by the development of these lands call for patience some early indications in the availability of bio-mass point to a bright future to come. People having lands in the rural areas are becoming increasingly dependent on their own resources for fuel and fodder supplies. The fuelwood and fodder purchases from the markets in case of Tarai areas have come down easing the economic burden for the landed class. The improvement in the availability of supplies of these two variables on the government and community lands have also benefited the landless class. But fuelwood and fodder collectors are not in any better position as compared to the period before the start the social/farm forestry programmes in the area under investigations. Although a general consciousness regarding the need for improvement of eco-systems for the salvation of the rural people is raised in the areas under study, many people are still not very informative. The most concerned class is the rural women who still suffer a lot especially in the collection of fuel and fodder. The rural women feel that they are overburdened through the collection process of these important outcome components of the programmes undertaken on the wasted lands.

The respondents representing the Hill areas as revealed by the investigations have not participated in the owned wastelands development programme. In the Tarai area, 22 landed class respondents (about 8 per cent of the total) have reported their involvement in the wasteland development programmes. A total of 25 acres (1.19 acres per household) wasteland was developed for the purpose of fuelwood plantations, fodder and field crops introduction. A three-year data were recorded on the total expenses made and incomes received from the development programmes of these wastelands. According to the varied nature of the wastelands and their purpose of development, the expenses per year also vary. The various studies conducted on wasteland tracts of the country conclude different results. To summarize, the cost of reclamation depends on various factors like quality of the soil and its nutrient value, requirement of water and requirement of vegetation to be planted on it. Since, the prevention of degradation or the restoration of degraded lands yield benefits over many years, a time horizon of 10-12 is considered suitable for such analysis.[1] The National Bank for Agriculture and Rural Development (NABARD) expects a rate of return within 15 to 20 years of afforestation projects in wastelands.[2] The *usar* lands of Uttar Pradesh can be reclaimed for fuelwood afforestation at an expenditure of Rs.10,000 per hectare, at a benefit-cost ratio of 2.8, the pay back period will be ten years. The estimated cost of reclamation of Chambal ravines comes to Rs 5,000 per hectare at 4 benefit-cost ratio, the fuelwood plantations pay back period will also be ten years.[3] Considering the different qualities of wastelands, part of these can be reclaimed for agriculture and others can be put to growing fuelwood on any substantial scale. Estimates are that the reclamation of alkali soils of the regions of Uttar Pradesh, Haryana and Punjab will cost Rs. 5,325 per hectare to make them suitable for field crop production, at a benefit cost ratio of 1.29, the pay back period will be four years.[4]

Table 4.1 shows annual expenses made on land reclamation under the studied conditions.

TABLE 4.1: Annual Expenses Made on the Development of Wastelands in Tarai Area

Particulars	Period of development		
	I Year	II Year	III Year
Total expenses incurred (Rs)	23,100.00	18,000.00	18,350.00
Mean	1,050.00	818.18	834.09
Std. Dev.	676.4755	543.6967	695.2879
Variance	457,619.0476	295,606.0606	483,425.3247
N	22	22	22

Chemical fertilizers have been the main items of expenditure for the development of wastelands during the first three-year period. These are followed by costs of seeds and saplings. Most of the labour used for land development comes from the family itself and its computed value have not been taken into account. Considering the reclamation cost very high elsewhere in the State its value for the reported period has been very low in the area under study. This is because the lands are not extremely either sodic or alkaline in nature. With sufficient availability of groundwater in the Tarai area, providing irrigation for reclamation is not a factor but high cultivation costs are naturally an additional burden to the pockets of the poor farmers.

The development of these barren lands, lying vacant for a long time, have paid dividends to their owners. A mixed cultivation of field crops with fuelwood plantations was experimented. Field crops have started giving incomes from the very first year while plantations of fuelwood species remain in tact in the fields after the harvest of the annual crops. Eighteen growers (82 per cent of the total farmers who have participated in the land development programme) have reported the incomes from these lands from the first year onwards. Table 4.2 shows the income received from crop production on the reclaimed lands.

TABLE 4.2: Incomes Received for the First Three Years from the Reclaimed Wastelands in Tarai Area

Particulars	Period of development		
	I Year	II Year	III Year
Total income received (Rs.)	19,100.00	27,600.00	32,100.00
Mean	1,061.11	1,533.33	1,783.33
Std. Dev	655.4198	835.2527	1,033.1277
Variance	429,575.1634	697,647.0588	106,752.9412
N	18	18	18

Although income received through the development of per unit of wasteland shows lower return, it has already started showing an increasing trend. Land improvement takes five to seven years to achieve land productivity at a level equal to the lands which are already under cultivation in the nearby areas. The above results are impressive and with these it can easily be assumed that the wasted lands in the study area can gain productivity in due course.

Land development provides a sizable employment to the family members of the farmers. The nature and extent of employment depends on the quality of land being developed. Table 4.3 gives the additional employment record for the households involved in the land development programme under the area of investigations.

Fuelwood plantation in Tarai area have been planted both on the agricultural as well as on wastelands by the growers. The most common practice has been to grow trees on the boundaries of the fields. In some of the cases (3 growers) the plantations have been grown under the block pattern. In both the cases, the growers were more interested to count the number of plants they have planted rather than the acreage under the plantation. Eucalyptus, shisham and babool are the main species of wood more common in the Tarai belt used for plantations, on the wastelands conditions. Table 4.4 shows the total number of plants raised during the social/farm forestry programme by the farmers.

TABLE 4.3: Employment Generated through Land Development Programme in Tarai Area

Particulars	Annual employment generated	
	Men	Women
Total days	895	565
Mean	44.75	33.23
Std. Dev.	25.8271	23.7132
Variance	667.0395	562.3162
N	20	17

TABLE 4.4: Number of Trees Raised on Agricultural and Wastelands by the Growers in Tarai Area

Particulars	Agricultural	Wastelands
Total trees raised	7,980	2,120
Mean	228	193
Std. Dev.	258.9095	153.8890
Variance	67,034.1176	23,681.8182
N	35	11

As is observed from the above table, farmers have planted more trees on agricultural lands as compared to wastelands. Thirty-five of these farmers have reported that they have planted about 8,000 trees on the field boundaries around agricultural lands. Only 11 farmers mentioned about the 2,120 plants they have raised on the wastelands.

Three farmers reported that they have sold fuelwood amounting to Rs. 4,100 from the plantations raised on the agricultural lands. Only one farmer mentioned an income of Rs. 500 through fuelwood selling from the reclaimed wastelands production.

The total cost of fuelwood plantations raised on owned land both on agricultural as well as on wasted lands are given in Table 4.5.

TABLE 4.5: Total Cost Incurred on Fuelwood Plantations in Tarai Area

Particulars	Agricultural Lands	Wastelands
Total cost (Rs.)	28.875	7,700
Mean	849.26	700.00
Std. Dev.	762.1363	536.6563
Variance	580,851.7157	288,000.0000
N	34	11

Raising plantations both on the agricultural as well as on wastelands have generated extra employment to the reporting households. Both the sexes have reported about the additional work they have enjoyed through the raising of plantations. Tables 4.6 and 4.7 show the employment generated on the growing of a plantations.

TABLE 4.6: Employment Generated Through Plantations on Agricultural Lands in Tarai Area

Particulars	Men	Women
Total days	735	405
Mean	25.34	20.25
Std. Dev.	11.4120	9.7973
Variance	130.2340	95.9868
N	29	20

TABLE 4.7: Employment Generated Through Plantations on Wastelands in Tarai Area

Particulars	Men	Women
Total days	290	214
Mean	26.36	19.45
Std. Dev.	11.4217	14.5146
Variance	130.4545	210.6727
N	11	11

Plantations grown on own fields, in the Hill areas also provide substantial employment to the growers. In Hill areas, as compared to Tarai area, women folk are more involved in the cultivation practices of fuelwood plantations. In the majority of cases, the plantations raised in the Hill areas are neither grown in compact blocks nor on the field boundaries but the trees are scattered all over the plot area on the slopes. This besides the production of biomass saves the soils from erosion. The people in the Hill areas are very well known to the practices and they are expert in raising the plantations of the mountainous sloppy and shallow upper soils. Table 4.8 gives the days of employment earned through these plantations.

TABLE 4.8: Own Farm Employment Generated Through Plantations in the Hill Areas

Particulars	Men	Women
Total days	300	1,370
Mean	14.29	23.62
Std.Dev.	6.9437	11.6902
Variance	48.2143	136.6606
N	21	58

The major economic activity in the rural areas through social forestry programmes has been the availability of employment to the local people. These programmes have provided the substantial job opportunities to the rural population for both the sexes. Development of wastelands, government vacant lands, community barren lands, have been covered in these programmes for the plantation process. Forest Department also provide casual jobs to the locals for development of eco-systems under its own set up. Railways, Public Works Department, Irrigation Department have been sources of temporary employment to the locals in raising plantations of land especially in the Tarai area. Although peoples participation in these activities have been very limited but have recently started attracting a large section of the rural population. Table 4.9 shows the number of days the local people were employed by various Departments in the raising of fuelwood plantations.

TABLE 4.9: Total Employment Generated Through the Plantation Development Programme on the Wastelands

Area/Source	Man days	Women days
Hills		
Forest Department	195 (10)	50 (1)
Community land plantation	440 (31)	310 (22)
Total	635	360
Tarai		
Forest Department	232 (13)	19 (2)
Community land plantations	288 (16)	24 (4)
Road side plantations	212 (15)	22 (2)
Canal side plantations	77 (6)	9 (1)
Railway side plantations	55 (3)	—
Other farmer's land plantations	382 (23)	33 (4)
Total	1,246	107

Note: Figures in parentheses show number of households worked on the plantations.

Women's participation, as compared to their partners in fuelwood plantations under the Hill areas is comparatively high. They account for about 36 per cent of the total work done. In the Tarai areas, their contribution has been only 8 per cent. These figures are apart from the total labour supplied for the same activities on their own farms. In Hill areas, the forestry programme has been more employment oriented as compared to the Tarai area. This is mainly because other job opportunities in the rural Hill areas are not available and more and more people are attracted towards cash payments. In the Tarai area, quite a large part of the labour force is diverted towards other employment outlets which are locally available in the intensive sugarcane producing area. However, the popularisation of forestry programme in recent years is becoming a potential employer to the local rural people in both the areas.

The rural people in the areas under study have been provided casual jobs in forestry programmes for various activities. Tables 4.10 and 4.11 give the details.

TABLE 4.10: Proportion of the Work Done by Rural People in Forestry Programmes in the Hill Areas

Worked at	Males	Females
Field preparations	33.51	15.91
Nursery development	6.28	0.85
Hole/ridge making	23.56	16.76
Planting	23.56	24.32
Manuring	—	0.57
Weeding	6.28	15.45
Irrigation/watering	—	—
Tree falling	4.24	6.62
Transportation	1.57	19.32
Total Labour	100.00	100.00

TABLE 4.11 Proportion of the Work Done by the Rural People in Forestry Programmes in the Tarai Areas

Worked at	Males	Females
Field preparations	38.04	31.50
Nursery development	10.39	12.60
Hole/ridge making	11.21	16.54
Planting	24.73	21.26
Manuring	0.95	2.36
Weeding	1.29	0.79
Irrigation/water	1.29	6.30
Tree falling	8.42	—
Transportation	3.67	8.66
Total labour	100.00	100.00

With the prospectus of the availability of casual employment in the social forestry programmes being carried out on wastelands in the area of study the wage rates, to some extent have been stabilized. Although a lower wage rate was reported by the respondents, many of them avoided to answer their total earnings through these programmes. Employment provided by the rural people for the community plantations in the Hill area was entirely on voluntary basis. Table 4.12 shows the per day wages earned through the forestry programmes in the rural areas.

TABLE 4.12: Daily Wages Earned Through the Forestry Programme

Sex/area	Responding Households	Rs. Per day
Males		
Hills	30	20.00
Tarai	58	17.68
Females		
Hills	14	15.00
Tarai	8	10.75

In the Hill areas, 45 workers have reported that they travel on an average upto 3.28 km to get the work in the forestry programmes. The distance covered by the Tarai villagers was 4.57 km from their respective villages.

The major impact of the wasteland/eco-system development in the Tarai area has been the coverage of more area under the plantations which has improved the local availability of fuelwoods. This situation is borne out by the fact that more outlets of fuelwood sale have come up in the Tarai area and its availability is comparatively better than in the Hills. A two point figures i.e, data collected for early 'eighties and for the present survey (1991-92) have indicated the following results.

The data shown in Table 4.13 are based on all the 90 respondents. Since fuelwood collection in the Hills is a women's enterprise, the travel up to the collection sites is a little over 2 kms each way, This distance has been maintained during the period of two sets of information collected. There is a sharp decline in the fuelwood collected, i.e. from 37.55 kgs. to 33.52 kgs, a decrease of about 11 per cent during a decade's period. The fuelwood collection time has shown a nominal increase of about 17 minutes per trip. This concludes that with the same distance of fuelwood available in the Hills the quantity being collected is reduced and it takes little more time to collect the fuelwood from the forest village wood lots. In other words, keeping the distance of fuelwood collection as a constant factor, the collection of one quintal of wood will need 15 hours in 1991-92 as compared to 11 hours 40 minutes about a decade ago. The increase in time may be mentioned as over 28 per cent/quintal/hour for two periods in the Hill area.

TABLE 4.13: Fuelwood Availability at Two Points in the Hills

Particulars	Early 'Eighties	1991-92
Distance of fuelwood collection		
Total distance covered (kms)	193	194
Mean	2.14	2.15
Std. Dev.	1.0338	1.1506
Variance	1.0688	1.3228
N	90	90
Quantity collected per trip		
Total quantity (kg)	3,380	3,017
Mean	37.55	33.52
Std. Dev	5.9608	5.6811
Variance	35.5306	32.2748
N	90	90
Time spent in fuelwood collection		
Total hours	433	458
Mean	4.81	4.08
Std. Dev.	1.0266	1.3209
Variance	1.0538	1.7448
N	90	90

Only five households have reported in the Tarai belt that they are involved in the fuelwood collection on the same pattern as the households in the Hill areas. For these households an increase of distance in the collection is reported to be about 0.2 kms i.e, from 3 to 3.02 kms, in two sets of data collections. Despite increase in the distance covered for fuelwood collection, its collected quantity also has improved i.e., from 31 to 40 kgs in a single trip. This increase is about 29 per cent in the quantity collected. The collection time per trip also has gone up from 3 hours 48 minutes to 4 hours 12 minutes, i.e., an increase of 0.53 per cent in time.

This can be concluded from these calculations that in the Tarai area less time is required to collect the same quantity of wood as compared to ten years ago. Thus, if distance is kept at a constant level, the decrease in time required to collect a given quantity of wood is less than 28 per cent/quintal/hour.

This further shows that while in the Hill areas about 28 per cent more time is required to collect a given quantity of wood, the same time is less required in the Tarai area. It may be concluded that due to massive afforestation programme in the Tarai belt as compared to the Hill areas, the overall availability of fuelwood has improved.

Following Tables show the details of fuelwood collection both at the Hills and Tarai areas.

TABLE 4.14: Distance of Fuelwood Collection by Females in the Hill Areas

Distance (km)	Early 'Eighties		1991-92	
	Households	Percentage	Households	Percentage
1-3	77	85.6	78	86.7
4-5	13	14.4	12	13.3
Total	90	100.00	90	100.00

TABLE 4.15: Fuelwood Quantity Collected in a Single Trip by Females in the Hill Areas

Quantity (kgs)	Early 'Eighties		1991-92	
	Households	Percentage	Households	Percentage
1-25	5	5.6	8	8.9
26-30	12	13.3	40	44.4
31.35	29	32.2	19	21.1
36-40	21	23.3	16	17.8
41-45	22	24.4	6	6.7
46 over	1	1.1	1	1.1
Total	90	100.00	90	100.00

TABLE 4.16: Time Spent in a Single Trip of Fuelwood Collection by Females in the Hill Areas

Time (hours)	Early 'Eighties Households	Early 'Eighties Percentage	1991-92 Households	1991-92 Percentage
1-3	2	2.2	—	—
4-5	67	74.4	59	65.6
6-7	18	20.0	26	28.9
Over 7	3	3.3	5	5.6
Total	90	100.00	90	100.00

TABLE 4.17: Distance of Fuelwood Collected* by Males in the Tarai Area

Distance (kms)	Early 'Eighties Households	Early 'Eighties Percentage	1991-92 Households	1991-92 Percentage
1-3	55	34.8	140	88.6
4-5	88	55.7	13	8.2
6-7	11	7.0	11	0.6
Over 7	4	2.5	4	2.5
Total	158	100.00	158	100.00

* Also includes purchases.

TABLE 4.18: Fuelwood Collected* in a Single Trip by Males in the Tarai Area

Quantity (kgs)	Early 'Eighties Households	Early 'Eighties Percentage	1991-92 Households	1991-92 Percentage
1-25	21	13.3	4	2.6
26-30	14	8.9	7	4.4
31-35	6	3.8	2	1.3
36-40	48	30.4	20	12.7
41-45	11	7.0	2	1.3
Over 45	58	36.7	123	77.8
Total	158	100.00	158	100.00

* Also Includes purchases.

TABLE 4.19: Time Spent in a Single Trip of Fuelwood Collection* by Males in the Tarai Area

Time (Hours)	Early 'Eighties		1991-92	
	Households	Percentage	Households	Percentage
1-3	7	4.4	42	26.6
4-5	34	21.5	70	44.3
6-7	48	30.4	39	24.7
Over 7	69	43.7	7	4.4
Total	158	100.00	158	100.00

* Also includes purchases.

The animals in the Hills are grazed on common lands and forests. The herbiage on the forest floor provides grazing in oak forests. In chir forests' the floor is burnt by the villagers in the spring of every year to remove the heavy litter of pine needles that tends to choke grass on growth. The rains that follow promote the growth of grass on which livestock graze, (Pine trees are ordinarily fire resistant). The livestock are also stall-fed but cattle feed is rarely purchased. The only fodder crop is barley and due to the scarcity of cultivable land, does not form a major part of animal diet. The main feeds are straw from the Kharif and Rabi crops, hay made from grass cut from the margins of fields, private plots, common lands and pine forests, and leaves lopped from several broad leave species of trees. The most important of these species are oak and Bhimal, found mostly in the forests besides private owned groves. These species are of special importance as they are the main sources of green fodder in the winter months. So common lands and forests are an important sources of food for livestock. Unlike Hills, the trees are not the source of cattle feed in the Tarai areas. The main cattle feeds in this belt are sugarcane tops (in the winter season), wheat and paddy straw, jowar and green fodder like *lucerne* and *berseem.* All these feeds are the products of cultivated lands. Besides this grazing on village common lands is also an important activity for the cattle raisers.

An impact of the wasteland development in the study areas can easily be observed on the production and availability of fodder. In the initial stage of development on the these lands, the plantations provide as a cover crops and fodder crops are sown/raised on the areas on reclaimed lands. In Hill areas, fodder-cum-wood trees like Bhimal (*Grewia oppositefolia*) were planted which have become the multipurpose trees to fulfil the needs of the local population. In the Tarai belt, many people as in the Hills, collect/reap grasses from the developed lands. This provides a substantial quantity of fodder supplies to the domestic animals. On a restricted basis the cattle are allowed to graze on the developed lands where plantations are still to grow. For the entire population of landless class in the Tarai areas and quite a large number of landed farmers in the Hills, grass collection has become a very popular activity for the local people. This activity is mainly pursued by the females in both the study areas. The unrestricted growth of grasses in the Hill areas and seasonal growth in the Tarai area are the major sources of domestic fodder supply. In the Hill areas, these are collected mainly from village community lands while in the Tarai areas besides community lands, government lands like, railway sides, road sides etc, provide the bulk of the quantity to meet the needs of the cattle.

Tables 4.20 and 4.21 show the sources of fodder supplies in the households.

As is reported, unlike fuelwood, fodder is not marketed in the Hill areas but some respondents are involved in this activity in the Tarai area. There is general increase in the availability of own farm production of fodder in both of the areas under study. The fodder collection from the forest have shown a decreasing trend while its collection from other sources have improved. These sources are mainly the village common lands and lands along with the road/railway sides. In Tarai area, non-agricultural class collects the sugarcane tops from the lands of other farmers thus increasing its supply in the total availability both quantitatively as well as for the number of respondents.

TABLE 4.20: Sources of Domestic Fodder Supplies in the Hill Areas

Sources	Early 'Eighties		1991-92	
	House-holds	Units	House-holds	Units
Own farm produce (Qtls)	29	385	32	400
Forest collection (Qtls)	4	85	—	—
Village land collections (Qtls)	79	2,390	85	2,781
Rail/road/canal side collections (Qtls)	—	—	11	210
Other farms collections (Qtls)	—	—	1	15
Average distance of collection (kms)	80	2.00	84	1.96
Time spent in a single collection (hours)	79	2.59	83	2.60
Average grazing area covered (kms)	64	3.25	85	3.48
Cattle grazed (Nos.)	65	232	82	284

TABLE 4.21: Sources of Domestic Fodder Supplies in the Tarai Area

Sources	Early 'Eighties		1991-92	
	Households	Units	Households	Units
Own farm produce (Qtls)	60	2,500	60	3,000
Forest collections (Qtls)	1	50	1	70
Village land collections (Qtls)	61	2,220	61	2,730
Rail/road/canal side collections (Qtls)	13	275	13	370
Other farms collections (Qtls)	31	884	32	1,170
Average distance of collections (kms)	116	2.80	116	2.35
Time spent in a single collection (hours)	116	4.72	116	4.22
Average grazing area covered (kms)	5	6.20	3	4.66
Cattle grazed (Nos)	3	60	2	13
Fodder purchased (Qtls)	29	1,002	22	830

The impact of the programme on the collection of timber, stone chips, slippers, leaves, medicinal plants, etc., from the improved wastelands has not properly been observed. The collected data lack the sequences of reporter and the respondent of the households. There would have been positively some impact in the Hill areas, as people in this area are more dependent for these supplies from the forests or degraded wastelands. But due to lack of data it has not been possible to come to a conclusion. In the Tarai area, people are not involved in the above said activities and neither the wastelands provide such resources to the local population.

NOTES

1. D.C. Das, Benefits from Soil and Water Conservation Programme, *S.P.W.D. Seminar Proceedings*, New Delhi, 1984.
2. K.G. Venkataraman, Designing, Planning and Financing of Tree Projects over Wastelands, *S.P.W.D. Seminar Proceedings*, New Delhi, 1984.
3. A.N. Chaturvedi, Firewood Farming on Degraded lands, *U.P. Forest Bulletin*, # 50, Lucknow, 1985.
4. I.P. Abroal and P.K. Joshi, Economic Viability of Reclamation of Alkali Lands with Special Reference to Agriculture and Forestry, *S.P.W.D. Seminar Proceedings*, New Delhi, 1984.

5

SOCIO-ECONOMIC INPUTS IN DOMESTIC ENERGY CONSUMPTION

The rural energy consumption pattern and its impact on the environment has been getting importance at national and international level during the recent past. Various studies[1] on the subject have shown that the broad features of rural energy consumption pattern on a wider level are similar. There is a marked variation in the specific end-uses and energy forms region to region, and from micro-region to micro-region, representing different agro-climatic and eco-systems in the country. These broad conclusions bring out the need for carrying out energy assessment in the household sector considering the account of socio-cultural and economic variables, their relationship to the existing pattern of energy consumption so that the desired pattern of energy consumption can be worked out for a sustainable agriculture and rural development planning atleast at a micro level base. Further, with the massive afforestation programme in wasteland tracts and the integrated planning for meeting rural energy needs for subsistence requirement, the development can partially be tapped locally through these renewable energy resources.

The requirement of total energy in the household sector is effected by various factors as its contribution is regulated by a number of variables. These variables form the part of economic, sociological, cultural practices, awareness, technological innovations, innovation acceptance by the rural people, etc. Some of these variables are countable and can be measured under certain regulated or unregulated conditions while others are not. There have always been variations in energy use due to one or the other of these variables. This emphasizes the necessity to understand the existing pattern of energy consumption in the household. The earlier sections of this work described the sources of domestic energy and their utilization at the household level.

To study the possibilities of lowering or increasing the domestic energy input for a sustainable concept, an attempt has been made in this section on the relationships of total household energy consumption (hereafter called the 'dependent variable') and associated factors to regulate this consumption (hereafter called the 'independent variables'). Regression analysis on linear model was adopted for the whole exercise, dealing with the two districts and 260 cases covered under the project.

The collected physical data on fuelwood utilization were converted into energy terms by using energy conversion ratios. Values of independent variables were utilized in their original form. Following variables were counted for the computations:

1. *Dependent variable:* Total domestic energy use in the household sector in terms of Mega Joule (MJ)
2. *Independent variables:* These variables were divided into three groups.
   (i) Economic variables.
   (ii) Sociological variables.
   (iii) Technological variables.

The counted variables under the above heads were:

(i) Agricultural income of the household (Rs.)
(ii) Non-agricultural income of the household (Rs.)
(iii) Own farm fuelwood production (kgs).
(iv) Fuelwood collected from different sources (kgs).
(v) Household expenditure on family maintenance (Rs).
(vi) Size of the household (No. of persons).
(vii) Level of education in the household, i.e, number of household with above High School, upto High

School and illiterates.

(viii) Caste (upper castes and backward castes).

(ix) Households using improved *chulhas* (No).

All the economic variables under the analysis were judged with the socio-cultural variables individually. Thus the household incomes and the total fuelwood supply within the household altogether were produced separately with the size of household, literacy rate, caste factor, and type of the improved *Chulha* used for domestic food preparations. The above analysis is done in conjunction with the dependent variable for both the areas under investigations.

The results of Table 5.1 as computed from the multiple regression analysis indicate that the regression coefficients for the two variables, namely, size of the households and the value of non-agricultural incomes are significantly contributing to the total domestic energy use in the Hill areas (district Pauri Garhwal).

The Hill households have been influenced by the large size of remittances on the total energy use in the area. As has been observed in the earlier pages of this report, for quite a large number of households in the Hills, the increased family income is due to these sources affecting the overall domestic energy consumption. In the case of Tarai areas (district Lakhimpur Khiri), the value of simple '*r*' which is negative for non-agricultural incomes, shows its negative influence on the domestic energy needs. The impact of the individual variable on the total domestic energy consumption in the households of Tarai area is significant in the case of household size, fuelwood gathered and agricultural incomes. For the Tarai area, the individual regression coefficients of all the variables are significant. The value R^2 is 0.413 in the case of Hills, means that all independent variables in the equation contribute upto 41 per cent. Similarly, R^2 value for Tarai equation comes to 0.696, means their contribution is around 70 per cent of the total function.

Table 5.2 shows that in Tarai areas there is no correlation between own farm fuelwood supply and dependent variable – total domestic energy consumption, but the regression co-efficient of these two variables shows that own farms fuelwood supply variable contributes significantly to the dependent variable.

The simple '*r*' being not significant between these two variables might be due to the effect of other variables and when these effects were partialled out its own contribution becomes significant. Thus it can be concluded on these interpretations that correlation being significant or non-significant does not show the correct position of the variables; it is only through the weights of regression co-efficient, we can conclude whether the independent variables contribute significantly or not. The value of regression co-efficient for households having high school plus education level does not show any impact on the total energy consumption in both the areas under investigations. Independent variables are contributing 35 per cent in the Hills and 63 per cent in the Tarai to the total energy equation.

Results of Table 5.3 reveal that under the investigated households in both the areas, the level of education where it is upto high school standard, is significantly contributing towards greater use of domestic energy in the Tarai areas. In the Hills, although value of simple '*r*' is significant, regression co-efficient is not found significant. Under the equation, the independent variables are contributing 35 per cent in the Hills and 65 per cent in the Tarai area to the total function.

Table 5.4 shows the positive influence on the total domestic energy use in the illiterate households under Hill areas. The regression co-efficient value indicates that illiteracy is significantly contributing towards the higher energy use. This is unfortunately true that most of the women folk in the Hill areas are not educated and they are the chief media of domestic energy use in the household kitchens. Indirectly it will not be possible to reduce the level of domestic energy consumption unless these women groups are trained and educated. In the Tarai area, these two variables have not shown any significance for the regression co-efficient. The value of R^2 for Hills and Tarai shows the independent variables contribution to the equation of 38 per cent and 63 per cent respectively.

Figures given in Table 5.5 show that the contribution and impact of the improved *chulhas* on domestic energy consumption in both the areas under investigations is not seen. In the Hill areas, households do not have the facilities of these *chulhas* hence their impact on the overall analysis has shown negative influence. Although the smokeless *chulhas* (improved ones) are being adopted by a limited number of households in the Tarai area, this variable is not significantly contributing to the overall or individually on the total domestic energy use. Castes other than 'upper' are not in existence in the Hills, and thus the influence of caste composition is not observed in the analysis. The caste composition is available for the Tarai areas, but its impact and contribution to the total energy consumption in the households is negative. The annual expenses made on family maintenance are significantly contributing to the total energy consumption besides the impact of the expenditure on consumption is found significant in the households of the Tarai area. The impact of annual expenditure on the energy consumption does not have significant role in the Hill areas. The value of R^2 in the equation shows that independent variables contribute 36 per cent in the Hills and 65 per cent in the Tarai area, to the total function.

The Main Findings of the Preceding Discussions can be Summarized as:

(i) The fuelwood energy for domestic consumption in the Hill areas is very much affected by the non-agricultural incomes of the households. The higher incomes and particularly the remittances received by the households have higher level of domestic energy consumption in comparison to those households who are entirely dependent on farming resources.

(ii) Population pressure on the households play an important role on the total domestic energy consumption. Any additional person in the household will substantially require more domestic energy and will further be a heavy burden on the energy budget under the areas of investigations.

(iii) Illiterate households and household having person with education upto High School have been consuming more domestic energy in the Hills as compared to those households where education standard is higher than the High School. This shows that awareness among the educated families have gone up to conserve fuelwood in the area through the savings of this resource.

(iv) The popularisation of improved *chulha* programme, unfortunately has not been impressive in the area under investigations. These *chulhas* are not in use by the rural population. Thus the towering of energy consumption through this programme has been minimal.

(v) Farm incomes (both from crop production as well as livestock raising) have direct impact on the domestic energy consumption in the households of Tarai area. The higher the incomes from these sources more is the utilization of fuclwood for domestic purposes. Since farming is the main source of livelihood in the Tarai area, its higher incomes are more associated with energy utilization.

(vi) Households having education level upto High School consume more domestic energy in the Tarai belt. This also proposes that poor awareness and knowledge about fuel scarcity of the family members are responsible for higher energy use in the household of Tarai area.

(vii) The energy consumption for different caste groups have no direct impact on the quantity use. The results further emphasize that the negative values of caste structure are observed on the fuelwood needs where no differentiation is seen among the caste groups in the investigated households.

(viii) There have been more energy utilization for domestic purposes in the Tarai households where family consumption budget is high. This means that with the increase of total family expenditure in the households the domestic energy consumption also increases and *vice versa.*

TABLE 5.1: Determination of Domestic Energy Consumption

Independent Variables	Units	Dependent variable = Total Domestic Energy Consumption (MJ)					
		Hills			Tarai		
		Regression Coefficient	Simple 'r'	't' Value	Regression Coefficient	Simple 'r'	't' Value
1. House hold size	Nos.	0.35*	0.58	3.05	0.37*	0.73*	6.22
2. Own farm fuelwood supply	Kgs.	0.10	0.14	1.20	0.11*	0.01	2.48
3. Fuelwood gathered from outside	Kgs.	0.06	0.02	0.69	0.11*	0.43*	2.32
4. Agricultural income of the household	Rs.	0.07	0.35	0.75	0.53*	0.73*	8.14
5. Non-Agricultural income of the household	Rs.	0.32*	0.54	2.95	0.15*	-0.07*	2.89
	Constant		17,831.288			5,081.819	
	Multiple R			0.643			0.834
	R Square		0.413			0.696	
	N		90			170	

* Significant at 0.01 level

TABLE 5.2: Determination of Domestic Energy Consumption

Independent Variables	Units	Dependent variable = Total Domestic Energy Consumption (MJ)					
		Hills			Tarai		
		Regression Coefficient	Simple 'r'	't' Value	Regression Coefficient	Simple 'r'	't' Value
1. Households with High School + education level	Nos	0.09	0.16	1.02	0.10	0.46*	1.90
2. Own farm fuelwood supply	Kgs.	0.14	0.14	1.63	0.11*	0.01	2.20
3. Fuelwood gathered from outside	Kgs.	0.04	0.02	0.43	0.15*	0.04*	2.95
4. Agricultural income of the household.	Rs.	0.15	0.36*	1.58	0.74*	0.73*	11.93
5. Non-agricultural income of the household.	Rs.	0.50*	0.54*	5.35	0.26*	-0.07	4.81
	Constant		19,930.937			6,132.426	
	Multiple R		0.597			0.795	
	R Square		0.356			0.632	
	N		90.000			170.000	

* Significant at 0.05 level

TABLE 5.3: Determination of Domestic Energy Consumption

Independent Variables	Units	Dependent variable = Total Domestic Energy Consumption (MJ)					
		Hills			Tarai		
		Regression Coefficient	Simple 'r'	't' Value	Regression Coefficient	Simple 'r'	't' Value
1. Households upto High School education level	Nos	0.07	0.23*	0.82	0.20*	0.56*	3.52
2. Own farm fuelwood Supply	Kgs.	0.15	0.14	1.65	0.12*	0.01	2.46
3. Fuelwood gathered from outside.	Kgs.	0.47	0.02	0.53	0.15*	0.40*	2.97
4. Agricultural income of the household.	Rs.	0.16	0.35*	1.72	0.68*	0.73*	10.78
5. Non-agricultural income of the household.	Rs.	0.48*	0.54*	5.04	0.22*	-0.07*	4.24
	Constant	19,308.926				6,798.659	
	Multiple R	0.594				0.806	
	R Square	0.353				0.650	
	N	90				170	

* Significant at 0.05 level

TABLE 5.4: Determination of Domestic Energy Consumption

Independent Variables	Units	Dependent variable = Total Domestic Energy Consumption (MJ)					
		Hills			Tarai		
		Regression Coefficient	Simple 'r'	't' Value	Regression Coefficient	Simple 'r'	't' Value
1. Illiterate households	Nos.	0.21*	0.39*	2.24	0.10*	0.47*	1.94
2. Own farm fuelwood supply	Kgs.	0.12	0.14	1.32	0.11*	0.01	2.19
3. Fuelwood gathered from out side	Kgs.	0.02	0.02	0.22	0.15*	0.40	2.85
4. Agricultural income of the household	Rs.	0.11	0.36*	1.12	0.74*	0.73*	11.85
5. Non-agricultural income of the household	Rs.	0.46*	0.55*	5.01	0.26*	-0.07	4.24
	Constant		19,858.627			6,851.859	
	Multiple R		0.620			0.795	
	R Square		0.385			0.632	
	N		90			170	

* Significant at 0.05 level

TABLE 5.5: Determination of Domestic Energy Consumption

Independent Variables	Units	Dependent variable = Total Domestic Energy Consumption (MJ)					
		Hills			Tarai		
		Regression Coefficient	Simple 'r'	't' Value	Regression Coefficient	Simple 'r'	't' Value
1. Households using the improved Chulha	Nos.	-0.08	-0.15	-0.87	0.05	0.08	1.05
2. Upper Caste households	Nos.	–	–	–	-0.09	-0.29*	1.84
3. Own farm fuelwood supply	Kgs.	0.16	0.14	1.78	0.11*	0.01	2.27
4. Fuelwood gathered from outside	Kgs.	0.02	0.02	0.21	0.15*	0.40*	2.96
5. Agriculture income of the households	Rs.	0.13	0.35	1.21	0.46*	+0.73*	3.23
6. Non-agricultural income of the household.	Rs.	0.29	0.54*	0.99	0.18*	-0.07	2.74
7. Annual household expenditure on family maintenance	Rs.	0.23	0.56	0.73	0.30*	0.76*	2.29
	Constant		27,199.236			12,014.279	
	Multiple R		0.601			0.804	
	R Square		0.361			0.646	
	N		90			170	

* Significant at 0.05 level

NOTE

1. NCAER (1985) study of Indian conditions gives the details on the subject.

6

WOOD ENERGY DEVELOPMENT FROM THE VILLAGE WASTELANDS

The calculations of the foregoing sections show that fuelwood among the non-commercial sources is the main contributor of rural energy supply. It is the most important element in non-commercial energy in the household sector especially its use for cooking purposes by all the socio-economic groups in the villages. The empirical evidences show that in the rural surroundings of the study area of Uttar Pradesh Hills and Tarai belt, its contribution is about three-fourths to the total domestic energy requirements mainly for kitchen purposes.

Results of the many studies conducted on fuelwood surveys indicate that there has been a progressive rise in the consumption of this fuel source in the rural areas of the country.[1] This statement further strengthens the basic idea about fuelwoods and it can be concluded that those people who think that wood is a fuel of the past, should be aware that it has been gaining in importance steadily as a major source of energy for a majority of country's population. Since there are several economic, social and environmental advantages of fuelwood over other non-commercial sources of fuel, it is receiving greater attention both by the planners and its consumers. Unfortunately, the rapid population growth and the continuing dependence on fuelwood in the rural areas has led supply to fall too far behind the demand. The decreasing forests, increased intensity of floods and droughts have added to the shortages. The Advisory Board for Energy[2] in its report concludes that the fuelwood scenario for Uttar Pradesh in 2004-05 is not likely to meet the demand. In continuation, the Sixth Five-Year Plan outlined a detailed strategy for self-reliance in the energy sector. The Plan has made a special provision for the establishment of energy plantations and emphasis has been given to harnessing the sources of energy to meet the energy requirements of rural communities. Accordingly, the demand and supply position has shown that the gap is ever widening and productivity per unit area/time is very low. Thus to circumvent the situation and to satisfy rural energy needs, is to go in for a massive afforestation programme. To face the situation, the objective has to be that every village is able to meet its fuelwood, fodder and timber requirements by growing trees and shrubs on the available lands. As a matter of policy all the degraded government lands, Land Management Committee lands/forest lands be planted for the fast growing species of fuelwoods.

Raising fuelwood plantations on these lands have some complexities especially as regards the forests, the major fuelwood producer, in the State of Uttar Pradesh are concerned. To understand the forest produce scenario in general and fuelwood in particular in the State, we have to go back to the 'fifties.

With the merger of the princely States and abolition of the *Zamindari* system, the ownership of most of the forests land got transferred to the State and hence all the forest products have come under the State ownership. However the users for these products were still from the households, industry and government itself. Thus a peculiar relationship between a single producer and multiple users co-existed for a long period in post independence era.[3]

Under the above pattern although all the forest lands were under government control, certain forestry produce like fuelwood, fodder, small timber for rural housing and agricultural implements still came from the village common lands and farmer's own fields. And except for a rare cash transaction, the trading of these produce was not noticed. The largest proportion of these produce i.e., like fuelwood was not traded at all. With the increase of population growth, resulting in the increasing demand of these forestry produce, there has emerged the thinking for new energy resources that could help the deteriorating situation especially in the village atmosphere. This has led to the launching the idea of social forestry programme. Thus, under the programme new land areas are brought under tree cover and new producers for forestry products have entered/are entering the production system. Thus a major change in the production system has already started taking place.

Various studies conducted on the evaluation of the social forestry programmes in the country show that progress has been made in the afforestation on government lands along roads, canals, railways, on village common lands (LMC), and on private lands. While the plantations on government and LMC lands are done by the government agencies, the plantation on private lands is undertaken by farmers themselves. Unlike ownership, the produce from government lands are disposed of in the same manner as those from forest lands, i.e., government is both producer as well as owner of the land; private produce are entirely in the hands of farmers, i.e., they are both producers as well as owners of the lands. In the case of LMC lands where community is the owner of the lands, the details of the produce has to be worked out once the plantations raised thereon are at the stage of prime use. Many points at this juncture remain to be answered, like, disposal of the produce, retained quantity by the village community, storage, price structure, distribution within the community, etc.

At present, the daily fuel demands of the villagers under investigations are met by the surrounding forests, and or naturally grown wood masses either on the community lands or on government lands. While the former source is the only supply outlet to the villagers of Hills, the latter two forms the major contribution to fuelwoods in the Tarai belt. The pattern of forest resources is more or less the same for the two areas under investigations. A wide variety of forest types are found in Uttar Pradesh Himalayas – ranging from tropical forests to alpine meadows. The vegetational regimes are distributed from sal (*Shorea robusta*) dominated roughly at 300 m to 900 m in Tarai to chirpine (*Pinus roxburghii*) at 900 m to 1,800m. The main species from 1,800 m to 2,400 m is bani oak (*Quercus leucotrichophara*) giving way to other oaks from 2,400 m to 3,000 m. The main tree species above 3,000 m are the Himalayan spruce (*Abies smithiana*) and Himalayan silver fir (*Abies pindrow*), which occur alongwith pine meadows. There are considerable overlaps between the zones with, for example, oak going down to as low as 1,200 m in certain places.

Under the existing situation, the dry miscellaneous forests/wood are the principal sources of fuelwood yield where working system is simple coppice or its modification with 30 – 40 years rotation. Irrespective of very fast growing and excellent coppicing tree species, the output of forests is much less than its yield capacity. To pace with the time, for an increased productivity, there is need for sound planning in forest management in areas where energy trees and shrubs are to be established. It is not that no systematic pattern exists for the forest management in the area. In Uttar Pradesh Hills, there are at present three well recognised systems of forest management, namely, management of reserve forests by the Forest Department and management of Van Panchayat forests by the Van Panchayats (U.P.) and management of civil/soyam forests by the Gram Panchayats for and on behalf of the Revenue Department. The reserve forests are managed by the Forest Department using a bureaucratic-cum-technocratic approach in which forests are given more importance than the peoples basic needs while the Van Panchayats follow a people-oriented approach. The civil/soyam forests are in fact, not managed at all, in most cases, they are now lying barren and degraded wastelands.

In the Hill areas, the need for fuel fodder, etc. of a large part of the local population is fulfilled from the nearby reserved forests. Besides, the local people have limited rights of fuelwood, small timber and so on in the reserved forests. Over a time, these requirements of the people for forest produce have gone up tremendously but their rights have not been revised to cope with the increased requirements. Consequently, there have been reports at large, that people have started illicit felling (dry trees) and pilferage of the reserved forest produce.

The analysis of the forgoing sections shows that the fuelwood used for domestic purposes in the households under the studied areas consists more of branches/twigs (over 90 per cent of total use) than logs. In the majority of cases (over 95 per cent) dead trees are collected for domestic fuels. The cutting of entire trees as a matter of fact is not practised. This can be easily concluded that those farmers who have adopted the farm forestry plantations on their lands (strip as well as block plantations) have so far not started to cut the entire trees for their fuelwood requirements. In the studied area of Hills and Tarai, the lopping of trees, raised under plantations on forest lands; government lands/LMC lands/private lands, is a very common practice followed almost by all the households under investigations. On these grounds, this could easily be concluded that the majority of trees (*eucalyptus, shisham, acacias, pine, toona, bhimal,* etc.) planted under the forestry programme are being grown for sale rather than for domestic purposes. Alternatively, the farmers are awaiting the trees to be mature enough for extra biomass production from the trees.

According to the figures mentioned in section three of this study, about 89 per cent of the fuel needs of the households in the Hills and 97 per cent in the Tarai areas are met by self-collected dung cakes, crop residues, fuelwood etc. Among the Tarai households leaving apart one-fourth of fuelwood supplies from the markets, all the requirements are met by self-collection. Thus only a meagre amount is being spent on fuel needs through actual purchases. The observations reveal that the groups including small farmers/landless class/village poor hardly spent any rupee on their domestic fuel needs. Thus the main demand for fuelwood in the village is from such consumers who do not budget for fuelwood. They are benefited after the government and /or LMC lands are afforested. More trees on private lands only marginally help them, as their paying capacity is limited. This is against this background that forest lands in both the investigated areas are still being used by wood gatherers. The farmers turned tree growers are more concerned with their own consumption of fuelwood and incomes thereafter. On these grounds it can easily be assumed that the government lands including LMC lands and forest areas have to cater to the requirements of the majority of the villagers especially the lower strata of the society.

As stated earlier that most of the fuel requirement of the household is met by collection of drift wood. But there have been occasional instances when the villagers illegally cut trees to meet their fuel demands not met by drift wood collection. In some of the cases, the villagers are very selective in regard to tree cuttings. According to the figures given in section three, the fuel load borne by different tree species shows that *Pinus longifolia, Cedrela toona, Quercus incana, Grewia oppositifolia, Dalbergia sissoo, Acacias* and *Eucalyptus* suffer highest fuel load pressure in the two areas of investigations. This would mean that the exploitation of these tree species for fuel demands of the villages is continuing at more rapid rate than other tree species. The simple reason from villagers point of view appears that these tree species have got fast burning high energy yield properties and hence preferred by the villagers. They are specially suitable for providing domestic fuelwood requirement in the Hills and Tarai regions of the State.

Close observation and a careful survey of the studied villagers fuelwood needs have shown that the carrying capacity of the forests in Hill areas, to some extent, permits the accommodation of the local fuel pressure placed upon it. But the position in the Tarai belt is entirely different where very heavy pressure by the villages for the fuelwood needs is reported on the available wood lots/forests. In both the cases, although the proportion may be varied, the forest wealth is depleting fast. People in the Hills are more serious about the situation. They have switched the process of change in energy scenario and the dependence on commercial energy is growing (the reported use of commercial energy in the Hill areas comes to about eleven per cent). Today, when attempts are being made to adopt more and more renewable sources of energy, this reverse trend in the energy sector in the Hills needs to be halted. The position in the Tarai belt is different where agricultural/crop residues provide substantial amount of domestic energy needs. However, to undertake the massive programmes of planting fuelwood trees in the Hills has many constraints. First is the fragmented landholdings. A large number of villages in the Hill areas lack community lands and those who have it do not have sufficient land on an average for the purpose of plantations. Also all the available community lands are not good enough for fuelwood plantations. Thus large scale community plantations is not possible in the Hills. The irrigation is not possible in the Hills and thus to make use of groundwater is the only option. This warrants proper care in selection of fuelwood species besides heavy input of investments. The availability of community land is not so acute in the Tarai belt. Besides the area has sufficient surface and groundwater resources but land encroachment problem will make it difficult to get the required area for energy plantations.

Considering these constraints, it would be an appropriate decision that the villagers, in both the areas under investigations, who have their own land resources (irrespective of the quality of soils) be encouraged to establish their own forests for meeting their fuel requirements. This would to some extent reduce the energy collection pressure on the forest/government/LMC lands. Through this process a large proportion of the rural population will fulfil their fuelwood energy requirements by their own resources. Thus farm forestry programme besides social forestry be properly given weightage for the afforestation programmes. The agricultural operations in the studied areas are seasonal in character resulting in peak work periods. The farm family members, both males and females in the Tarai belt and females in the Hills, are able to find time in between the peak work periods which they can utilize for afforesting the fuelwood species on their own lands. Doing so the farmer families can utilize their intermittant hours of time for the growing of trees of their fuel needs for which the opportunity cost of the family labour would be zero. This will be without additional burden either on the family[4] or on land resources.

Land utilization data for the two studied districts show that 27,506 hectares (18,245 hectare in Pauri and 9,261 hectares in Khiri) might be available for raising fuelwood plantation on the wastelands. This area comes to about 15 per cent in Pauri and 79 per cent in Khiri of the total wastelands in the two districts respectively. Considering the local agro-climatical situation of the areas under investigations, this could easily be assumed that all the plantable area of 27,506 hectares be covered under suitable promising fuelwood species. The results of the various experiments conducted during the last two-three decades in the country suggests that with the available technology, these wastelands can be reverted back to their original productive conditions through re-afforestation programmes.

Experiments conducted at the High Altitude Plant Physiology Research Centre, located at Sri Nagar, under the HNB Garhwal University observe that the most promising fuelwood species suitable for the Hill areas are : *Dalbergia sissoo, Albizzia lebbek, Melia azedarach, Boehmeria rugulosa, Leucaena leucocephala.* These species, as shown in Table 6.1 have high survival and growth rates in the mountanous terrain.

TABLE 6.1: Results of the Selected Fuelwood Species at High Altitude Plant Physiology Research Centre, Sri Nagar, Garhwal

Species	Survival rate (after 2 Years)	Height in cm. (after One Year)
Dalbergia sissoo	89	51.5
Albizzia lebbek	65	60.2
Melia azedarach	79	41.5
Leucaena leucocoephala	70	66.9
Boehmeria regulose	78	97.6

Source : Dr.A.R. Nautiyal (1988)

For the Tarai belt, where results obtained on the basis of experiments conducted elsewhere in the plains and tropical climate could be applicable the most promising species for fuelwood cultivation are: *eucalyptus, Acacias, Dalbergia sissoo, Leucaena leucocephala, Prosopis juliflora*

For the cultivation of these species under the two areas of investigations, suggestion can be made considering the cost constraints and regarding the type of plantations that have to be grown. There are options that could be considered for the process

The experiences of high density agro-forestry (HDAF) show that high yield of fuelwood plantations are possible when they are planted with denser than conventional spacing and harvested on shorter than conventional cycles. The trees are allowed to make effective and maximum use of the entire plantation site, to remain sufficiently long to develop strong root system so as to permit repeated coppicing but they are not allowed to remain for unduly long time to compete with one another for space, sunlight, water and nutrients.

Plantations grown under the HDAF in parts of Maharashtra and Gujarat for *eucalyptus, Prosopis juliflora, Leucaena leucocephala, Melia azedarach, Techona grabdis* species have increased the plant population per unit area by 6 to 10 times as compared to conventional farm forestry.[5] At 60 cm × 60 cm spacing with 80 per cent survival rate, the bio-mass was ready for cutting after three years. This has an increase in bio-mass 3-5 times that obtained for spacing of 2m × 2 m commonly used in conventional farming. The grower points out that selective cutting can be started after 2 years 9 months and continuous cycle of cutting, the first one-third of trees are cut in fourth year followed by one-third every year. In the seventh year, trees first cut are ready for second cutting.

Considering the poor availability of fuelwood in the wastelands where situation is becoming more alarming to cope with energy supply to the growing population, the concept of HDAF could easily be adopted in the Hills and Tarai parts of Uttar Pradesh. The climate of Pauri district is not so hostile while in the Khiri district also, both climate and soils are most suitable for cultivation of fast growing fuelwood species on the pattern of HDAF. The cost component under the system where higher capital investment is required has to be met either through institutional financing or highly subsidized inputs including labour.

Against this background attempts could be made to chalkout an energy production programme on the existing land resources and for the year 2001. The parameters shown in Table 6.2 for the production of biomass and of the high yielding short rotation species having good coppicing capacity tested elsewhere have been adopted

TABLE 6.2: Fuelwood Yield for Some Promising Species

Species	Yield per tree (at 5 yrs age) (airdry basis kgs.)	Nos. of plants per ha	Fuelwood production (Tonnes/Ha/ 5 Year)
1. *Eucalyptus*	15.60	5,500	93.0
2. *Dalbergia sissoo*	15.00	6,515	82.0
3. *Acacia nilotica*	24.00	5,264	113.5
4. *Acacia tortilis*	27.90	4,995	117.0
5. *Prosopis juliflora*	35.00	5,917	167.0
6. *Albizzia lebbek*	25.09	4,400	66.0
7. *Cassia siamea*	34.00	2,611	85.0
8. *Leucaena leucocephala*	25.00	5,000	125.0
9. *Melia azedarach*	19.60	5,210	95.5
10. *Bochmeria rugulosa*	21.00	6,200	107.0
11. *Techoua grabdis*	16.50	5,000	98.0

Source: V.J. Patel (1988), M.P. Sharma (1988), S.N. Singh (1988) A.R. Nautiyal (1990), others.

As stated earlier, the plantation programme for fuelwood species mentioned above has to be taken up on priority basis at the farmer's level. To begin with, it is recommended that each landed farmer grows atleast 200 fuelwood trees under the farm forestry programme. This is in continuation of what few farmers in Tarai area have voluntarily grown fuelwood trees on their agricultural and wastelands. The number of such trees comes to 228 on wastelands and 193 on agricultural land per household (see Table 4.4). For the social forestry plantations, all the available LMC degraded lands should be covered under the fuelwood energy species. Fuelwood, thus grown under these systems will meet the entire demand of the local rural population. It is proposed that by the end of the century both the districts will be self-sufficient in their energy needs through fuelwood production. It is also expected that not only the entire population of the districts will locally be supplied the produce from the wastelands but there will be surpluses of a large marketable quantity of fuelwoods.

On these assumptions, a self-sustained programme for the availability of fuelwood by the year 2001 in the districts has been developed. The basic input data in the following analysis have been used from the secondary as well as primary sources.

TABLE 6.3: Basic Data of the Two Districts as Projected for the Year 2001

	Items	Pauri District (Hill areas)	Khiri District (Tarai areas)
1.	Total wastelands (ha)*	12,143,341	11,687
2.	Plantable wastelands (ha)*	18,245.38	9,261.60
3.	Plantable wastelands as percentage to total wastelands (%)	15.03	79.25
4.	Projected total population+	795,671	3,368,448
5.	Projected rural population	716,103	3,031,603
6.	Average size of the households in the rural areas **	6.53	7.93
7.	Total Number of households+	109,663	382,295
8.	Households with agricultural land (Nos)+	102,353	348,563
9.	Households without agricultural land (Nos)+	7,310	33,732
10.	Annual fuelwood consumption (kgs/household)++	2,423.30	2,213.54

Source: * Table 1.1.
** Table 1.3.
\+ Self calculations
++ Table 3.7. This has been assumed that fuelwood consumption at the household level in 2001 will be at the same. Hence no changeover in inputs have been considered.

TABLE 6.4: Total Bio-mass Production Through Farm Energy Forestry for the Year 2001

	Items	Pauri District (Hill areas)	Khiri District (Tarai areas)
1.	Fuelwood trees to be grown by each farmer (Nos)	200	200
2.	Fuelwood producing trees-1/3 annually (Nos)**	66	66
3.	Bio-mass production per tree annually (kgs)*	25	25
4.	Total annual bio-mass production per family (66x25) kgs	1,650	1,650
5.	Total biomass production in the district (kgs)	168,882,450 (102,353x1,650)	575,128,950 (348,563x1,650)

Note: * The computed average from Table 6.2. As proposed the bio-mass production under the HDAF pattern will be much higher than this yield. However, for a safer calculation the production per tree has been considered on a lower side.

** This is based on the criterion developed under the HDAF, where one-third trees are ready for harvest every year.

TABLE 6.5: Total Bio-mass Production Through Farm Energy Forestry for the Year 2001

	Items	Pauri District (Hill areas)	Khiri District (Tarai areas)
1.	Total plantable area (ha)*	18,245.38	9,261.60
2.	Area under 3 years bio-mass production cycle (ha)+	6,081.79	3,087.20
3.	Expected bio-mass, production (100 tons/ha/year)**	608,179	308,720

Source: * Table 6.3.

** The computed average from Table 6.2. This yield has also been taken on the lower side. Under the HDAF concept, the yields should be much higher for the mentioned species.

\+ This has been calculated on the criterion developed under HDAF pattern where one-third of the land area will be ready annually for bio-mass production.

TABLE 6.6: Annual Fuelwood Balance in 2001 Through Energy Forestry Programmes

	Items	Pauri District (Hill areas)	Khiri District (Tarai areas)
A. Farm Forestry			
1.	Total own farm production (tonnes)	168,882	575129
2.	Total consumption on farming households (tonnes)	248,032	771,558
3.	Balance (tonnes)	-79,150	-196,429
4.	Balance per household (kgs)	-773.30	-563.54
5.	Production as percentage to consumption (%)	68.09	74.54
6.	Consumption as percentage to production (%)	146.87	134.15
B. Social Forestry			
7.	Total production from community land (tonnes)	608,179	308,720
8.	Total consumption on non-farming households (tonnes)	17,714	74,667
9.	Balances (tonnes)+	+590,465	+234,053
10.	Balance after deducting the shortfall of farming household (tonnes)+	+511,315	+37,624

As mentioned in the above tables, social energy forestry has to be developed at all the degraded and plantable LMC lands while farm energy forestry by all the individual farmers. According to these suggestions, growing of a moderate number of 200 fuelwood trees per landed household will not be a difficult exercise for such a needy bio-mass programme in the area. Fuelwoods thus produced from the farm energy forestry will support only two-thirds supply of the fuelwood needs of the farming community. The rest of the fuelwood requirements, as is expected, will come from the produce grown on the degraded village common lands. These assumptions are based on that there is no change in the size of the household and major technological innovations is saving the non-conventional energy are not being adopted by the rural people. An overall picture by 2001 emerges that the two districts under the investigations will have surplus supplies in fuelwoods. The total marketable quantities of the fuelwoods in 2001 will be approximately 511,315 tonnes in Pauri Garhwal district and 37,624 tonnes in the Lakhimpur Khiri district.

NOTES

1. The per capita fuelwood consumption in rural India at two points survey conducted by the NCAER were 119.6 kgs. in 1975-76 and 153.1 kgs. in 1978-79 in the northern region of the country. According to the present investigations, the per capita consumption comes to 313 kgs. in Hill areas and 270 kgs. in Tarai belt of Uttar Pradesh.
2. Government of India, The Advisory Board on Energy, New Delhi, 1985.
3. The introduction of social forestry programme in the country has recently changed the equation and more results are still awaited.
4. According to government planning, the saplings of fuelwood species are available on highly subsidized rates in the nurseries maintained by the Forest Department.
5. V.J. Patel (1988)

BIBLIOGRAPHY

Bantley, B., The Uncultivated Half, USAID Report, Ford Foundation, New Delhi, 1984

Chaudhry, Kamla, *Wastelands and the Rural Poor*, New Delhi, 1987.

Chopra, S.K., Survey of Indian Agriculture, *The Hindu*, Madras, 1988.

Dewan, M.L., *Peoples Participation in Himalayan Eco-Systems Development*, Concept, Publishing Company, New Delhi, 1989.

Dobhal, G.L., *Development of Hill Areas*, Concept Publishing Company, New Delhi, 1986.

Food and Agriculture Organisation, Wood Fuel Surveys, Rome, 1983.

Food and Agriculture Organisation, A New Approach to Domestic Fuelwood Conservation: Guidelines for Research, Rome, 1986

Government of India, Indian Agriculture in Brief, 20th Edition, Ministry of Agriculture, New Delhi.

Government of India, The Advisory Board on Energy, New Delhi, 1985.

Government of Uttar Pradesh, *Statistical Bulletin*, District Khiri, 1989.

Government of Uttar Pradesh, *Statistical Bulletin*, District Pauri Garhwal, 1989.

Government of Uttar Pradesh, Eighth Five-Year Plan and District Sector Plan, Economics and Statistics Office, Khiri, 1990.

National Council of Applied Economic Research, Domestic Fuel Consumption in Rural India, New Delhi, 1965.

National Council of Applied Economic Research, Survey of Rural Energy Consumption in Northern India, New Delhi. 1978.

National Council of Applied Economic Research, Domestic Fuel Survey with special reference to Kerosene, New Delhi, 1985.

National Wasteland Development Board, Wasteland Development Programme-Guidelines for Action, New Delhi, 1985.

National Wastelands Development Board, First Meeting of the National Land Use and Wastelands Development Council, New Delhi, 1986.

Nautiyal, A.R., *Salient Features on the Progress of Energy Plantations Project*, HNB University, Sri Nagar 1990.

Patel, V.J., *A New Strategy for High Density Agro-Forestry*, Jivarajbhai Patel, Agro-forestry Centre, Kardej, Gujarat, 1988.

Planning Commission, Report of the Fuelwood Study Committee, New Delhi, 1982.

Sharma, M.P., Proceedings of Bio-Energy Society of India, New Delhi, 1988.

Sharma, R.D. *Economics of Fuelwood Production in Wastelands*, Concept Publishing Company, New Delhi, 1992.

Singh, S.N., Proceedings of Bio-Energy Society of India, New Delhi, 1988.

Society for Promotion of Wasteland Development, *Wasteland News*, Various Volumes, New Delhi.

Society for Promotion of Wasteland Development, Economics of Wasteland Development, *SPWD/NABARD Seminar*, New Delhi, 1984.

University of Garhwal, Himalayan Nomads; Traditions, Transition and Environment, Report Deptt. of Political Science, Sri Nagar, 1989.

Vimal, O.P. and P.D. Tyagi, *Bio-Energy from Wastelands*, New Delhi, 1986.

INDEX